"*Beyond My Church* is a thought-provoking and honest challenge to much that is taken for granted in our present church culture. Jason Dukes presents us with another way that is both biblical and practical. His stories and examples are fresh and engaging. If you are tired of business as usual with churches on every corner of your town doing their own thing with no regard for each other, then this book is for you!"
—Rick Morton, discipleship pastor, Temple Baptist Church, and coauthor of *Orphanology: Awakening to Gospel-Centered Adoption and Orphan Care*

"As a new church planter I battled the temptation to work mainly for my church. Thankfully, God reconnected me with one of my childhood heroes as we began to establish the foundational DNA of our new church family. Jason inspired me with many of the conversations found in this book and it reshaped my philosophy of life and ministry. Thanks, Jason, for being my friend and living out the words in this book!"
—Rob Wilton, lead pastor, Vintage Church

"In *Beyond My Church*, Jason Dukes challenges us not to be *a* church, but be *the* church in our communities. I love what the unity of believers in one community communicates to people and how Jason challenges us toward that vision. This book excites me about how the church can change a community by helping people so they can see our love for God and others."
—Dave Ferguson, lead pastor, Community Christian Church; spiritual entrepreneur, NewThing

"This book resonates, makes you pause, think, reflect, smile, laugh, and also self-examine as you shift uneasily in your seat—because it goes to the heart of issues about contemporary, comfortable 'church' and how it has moved away from the early church described in Luke's Book of Acts."
—Bill McCall, global economist, McCall & Partners

"It only stands to reason that if our Lord has the whole world in His hands, we should have the whole world on our hearts. Jason reminds us well of what it means to live the kingdom life."
—Dr. Johnny Hunt, pastor, First Baptist Church Woodstock

"Jason Dukes shares transformational lessons for the church that are born out of the real life that he has experienced with others who seek God's prescribed unity for the church. Such others-mindedness and sacrificial living create an environment through which Christ is more fully understood and embraced. Studying this book will challenge the reader's concept of church on many levels. This road is not an easy one, but the journey is necessary and truly profitable. Jason Dukes articulates what such unity looks like and how we can get there. May our Father's kingdom come."
—Gary Irby, director, Seattle Church Planting

"Jason Dukes is the real deal. And his vision for the unity (as well as the universality) of the church in mission is as visionary as it is practical. We need more of this in our time."
—Alan Hirsch, activist and coauthor of *The Forgotten Ways: Reactivating the Missional Church*

"*Beyond My Church* is the first book I've read that talks about how we, the church, can be the answer to Jesus' prayer found in John 17. Jason has articulated what a lot of us are feeling in our hearts could happen if we believed and practiced just the simplest commands of Jesus. Jason is truly a theo-practitioner. . . . I've seen him implement what he shares in *Beyond My Church*, and these aren't theories but values that he lives by personally, at home, in business, and through his church family."
—Billy Mitchell, Sun Coast Baptist Association

"Jason Dukes is one of the most purehearted missional leaders I know. His passion for God combined with sound missional thinking is a gift for the church. I highly recommend this."
—Jon Tyson, coauthor of *Rumors of God*

"Jason Dukes dreams with the best of leaders, researches with the best of students, discovers principles with the best of theorists, and facilitates learning with the best of teachers. But he refuses to stop in that world of hypotheses and ideas. As he searches for words from God for the church in our day, he actually puts them into practice. This he does in his own life and in the life of the church where he serves. Innovation and conviction stand, not as combating enemies, but arm in arm as partners in Jason's world. As you read his words, you can know they have come from our real Father, and been tested in the real world. Enjoy!"
—Randy Millwood, church planter and author of *To Love and to Cherish from This Day Forward . . . A Portrait of a Healthy Church*

"The 'MY church' mentality has manifested into a form of a church that is not ultimately one that missional nor Christ edifying. Jason Dukes will challenge you to rethink the church and to live as a sent one. We are sent ones called to embrace a grander and higher dream—a gospel movement much bigger than ourselves and much more powerful."
—Dr. Tiffany Smith, missions mobilization, Southern Baptists of Texas Convention

"Jason Dukes will challenge you to think differently about church. Not just differently, but biblically. Over the centuries, we've allowed the barnacles of tradition to grow on the hull of the church and without regularly scraping, the church has become almost unrecognizable. It is time to get down to the hull and rediscover what church is really supposed to look like. *Beyond My Church* is the scraper that will get you there."
—Mark Weible, director of church planting, Greater Orlando Baptist Association

"This book paints a beautiful picture of the way forward for the church in the Western world. Every follower of Christ should read it and begin living it out in the grace that Jason wrote it.'"
—David Putman, author of *Detox for the Overly Religious* and founder of plantingthegospel.com.

JASON C. DUKES

beyond MY Church

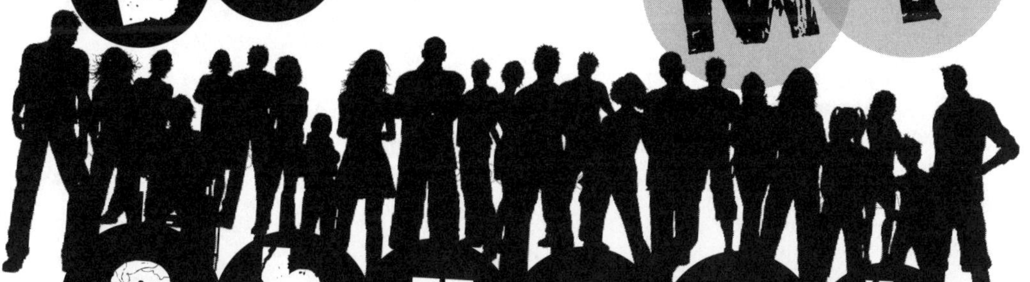

Thinking And Living So That The World Might Know

Birmingham, Alabama

New Hope® Publishers
P. O. Box 12065
Birmingham, AL 35202-2065
www.NewHopeDigital.com
New Hope Publishers is a division of WMU®.

© 2011 by Jason C. Dukes
All rights reserved. First printing 2011.
Printed in the United States of America.

No part of this publication may be reproduced, stored in a retrieval system, or transmitted in any form or by any means—electronic, mechanical, photocopying, recording, or otherwise—without the prior written permission of the publisher.

Library of Congress Cataloging-in-Publication Data
Dukes, Jason C.
  Beyond my church : thinking and living so that the world might know / Jason C. Dukes.
      p. cm.
   ISBN 978-1-59669-345-6 (sc)
  1. Community--Religious aspects--Christianity. 2. Interdenominational cooperation. 3. Mission of the church. I. Title.
  BV625.D85 2011
  248.4--dc23
                              2011038719

Scripture quotations marked *The Message* are taken from *The Message* by Eugene H. Peterson.
Copyright © 1993, 1994, 1995, 1996, 2000, 2001, 2002. Used by permission of NavPress Publishing Group.
  Scripture quotations marked NASB are taken from the New American Standard Bible®, Copyright © 1960, 1962, 1963, 1968, 1971, 1972, 1973, 1975, 1977, 1995 by The Lockman Foundation. Used by permission.
  Scripture quotations marked NLT are taken from the *Holy Bible*, New Living Translation, copyright © 1996. Used by permission of Tyndale House Publishers, Inc., Wheaton, Illinois. All rights reserved.

ISBN-10: 1-59669-345-2
ISBN-13: 978-1-59669-345-6

N124150 • 1211 • 3M1

to
my
dad
and
my
brother
for
modeling
the
beyond
ME
life

Other New Hope books
by Jason C. Dukes

Live Sent: You Are a Letter

Cartas Vivas (Spanish-language *Live Sent*)

A Thank You Note

It was my friend Erick Bauman who challenged me over coffee to have the courage to think and live this way.

We were enjoying coffee and friendship together.

We were conversing and asking a lot of what ifs. We had been somewhat cultivating "beyond MY church" in the city where we live, but our conversation and his encouragement pushed me to make unity among local churches a significant priority for our local church expression and to challenge other leaders in our area to make it a priority too.

Thank you, Erick, for challenging me in that way.

Table of Contents

13   **a silly intro about a serious subject**
think beyond "MY church" since it's not your church anyway

21   **chapter one**
drop the "MY church" mentality because Jesus' intentions were beyond that

35   **chapter two**
you matter in His mission, no matter what you think or what the pastor says

47   **chapter two-b**
you don't matter as much as you sometimes think, though

55   **chapter three**
am I addicted to MY church?

75   **chapter four**
am I cultivating for "on earth as it is in heaven" in our city or just trying to add members to MY church?

89 **chapter five**
  thinking and living beyond MY church with my family

107 **chapter six**
  thinking and living beyond MY church with my neighbors

121 **chapter seven**
  thinking and living beyond MY church in our city

137 **chapter eight**
  thinking and living beyond MY church together with other local church expressions

159 **chapter nine**
  thinking and living beyond MY church to the world

171 **chapter ten**
  moving beyond MY to HIS and US from here on out

Introduction

a silly intro about
a serious subject

> think beyond "MY church" since it's
> not your church anyway

It's not about you—wait, that line was used already, to start a book about purpose and life and driving. But it worked, you know? I mean, a gazillion billion copies later and it's still a good line. And a good book. I know a lot of people who were driven to it and have driven better since (in their daily lives). But just your life, purpose, and how you drive is not the purpose of *this* book. Although, after reading this lame opening paragraph, you are probably wishing you had not driven to the bookstore to get it. Or to your local cafe to download and read it online for that matter. Or whatever method you chose to buy it and read it. If you still choose to. So let's start over.

It's not about YOUR church. And it's not about MY church either. In fact, just calling it "your church" or "my church" is a bit arrogant, don't you think? Even saying that phrase seems to steal a bit of the ownership from the One who started this movement of people we now call "church." He is the Head of the church, after all. It's *His* church. Or better said, *we*, not it, are *His* church.

Do you think that? If so, can I ask a probing question? Then why do you think so much of church culture in America focuses on "their" own church's growth and success? Another question. Why do you think so few local church expressions include unity among the local churches in their city as a part of their overall strategy? One more question (at least for now). Do either of these last two questions describe the church family you call your own?

OK. Some more questions—this book asks a lot of them.

When is the last time:

you prayed for another local church in your community?

you heard the pastor or a leader highlight something another local church was up to?

that the local church expression you consider yourself to be a part of asked for more money to be given or raised but it wasn't for the local church expression you consider yourself to be a part of; it was instead for someone else?

You might think, *But I am not the pastor or on the pastoral team. I can't really affect change for a focus on more unity with other followers in our city.* To use a very sophisticated phrase my dad used some when I was growing up—BOLOGNA. That's pronounced [bah-low-nee] for those of you who may have moved beyond and long forgotten the fried bologna sandwich years like I have. We will dedicate a whole chapter to that line of thinking.

You might say,

"But why does this thinking beyond MY church stuff matter? Isn't it enough to focus on our own issues? We have enough and don't really care what the other churches do in our city."

To that I ask you, what if it matters to Jesus? What if He cares?

First, why does this matter—a.k.a. what's the purpose of this book? Here is the purpose, short and sweet:

To challenge you to think "beyond MY church" so that the work of God might happen in our cities and in our world.

I am coming at you with an acronym. You ready? TEST DRIVE A BMW. I know it's a long one. But don't you want to test drive a BMW? At least a convertible? It will help you remember the purpose of this book. It will help you and me remember that *your* church is not *your* church but *His* church. It will help you and me remember what Jesus wants us to remember about His work and His church. I would suggest that Jesus wants us to remember to:

Think beyond "MY church."
Envision unity among His followers in our city.
Strategize for the actual work of God in our city.
Talk about in our own gatherings what other local expressions in our city are doing.

Decentralize the efforts of the church in our city beyond Sunday mornings.
Release the church as a whole rather than relying so much on the clergy.
Invest into our city where the people are rather than just inviting them to where we are.
Visit with city leaders and ask them how the church together could serve our city.
Evaluate our success as the church by how we send rather than how many gather.

A (this letter stands for the letter *a*)

Blossom into a together-generosity as we cultivate the gospel together daily.
Multiply into new expressions as we grow in our unity.
Witness on earth as it is in heaven.

There you go. Now, I am fully aware of the fact that you will not remember the sentences that go along with that acronym. But at least you will remember the acronym, which will remind you of this book, which will remind you to pick up the book, which will allow you to read it again, which will remind you of the purpose of this book, which will compel you to think and live beyond MY church. Sounds like the children's book, *If You Give a Mouse a Cookie*.

Oh yeah. One more acronym. We need to remember all this and act on it NOW!

No more acronyms
Or else I
Will quit reading this book and never, ever, ever read anything you write again. For real though, seriously, don't you want to:

~ be involved in the work of God?

~ see the work of God around you?

Don't you want it:

~ to happen in more than just your church family?

~ to happen beyond "MY church" and instead come alive throughout our city?

In John 6:29, Jesus declared what the work of God is.
Jesus answered and said to them, "This is the work of God, that you believe in Him whom He has sent."
John 6:29 NASB

And in John 17, Jesus prayed for unity so that the world would believe in the One who was sent. We will unpack this more in the next chapter, but suffice it to say that it is not speculation to therefore conclude that unity among local church expressions is essential if we hope for the work of God to happen in our cities.

Thinking beyond MY church matters because the unity of the church is imperative in order for the work of God to happen in our city and in our world.

And I don't just mean unity in the one local church family that you call your own. I mean all followers of Jesus loving one another like Jesus loved us

~ so that the world will see us living His ways rather than our own

~ and believe that Jesus was sent as the Son of God because the kind of unity Jesus prayed for that should be lived out among His followers could only happen when God is the force holding us all together.

Please reread that last paragraph if you have to, because it is the point of this book. And please reread the BMW acronym if you have to, because whether you are labeled as clergy or laity (neither term am I fond of),

~ if you are a follower of Jesus,

~ then you matter as His church

~ as an integral part of His work

~ in our cities and in our world!

Thinking beyond MY church matters.

We asked another question at the beginning of this diatribe.

Does thinking beyond MY church matter to Jesus?

Yes. Simply put, it matters to Him because it's not your church, it's His. Read Matthew 16 and Romans 12 and 1 Corinthians 12 and Ephesians 4. You don't have a church. You have a church *family*, *a local expression* of His church—a people following Jesus together—with whom you are to love and unite and serve and make disciples and multiply, and with whom you are *not* to argue personal agendas or fight to preserve what you have or become isolated, caring nothing for other local expressions in the city.

Thinking beyond MY church also matters to Jesus because He does not see that one local expression you are so proud and protective of as the center of His kingdom. So you shouldn't either. In fact, He sees each local church expression as a sentence in the grander story that He is writing about His near and accessible love. And if the world does not see those who call themselves His followers as near to one another and accessible to our city, then they will not read that amazing letter of His love that He wrote not on stone tablets but on the hearts of people who follow Him together—His church. (For more on that metaphor, I encourage you to read *Live Sent: You Are a Letter.*)

So, if Jesus cares so much about each of His local expressions of His church, then maybe each of us should too. Maybe we should

~ strive for unity,

~ pay attention to what each expression is up to,

~ celebrate it and support each other,

~ put the interests of other local church expressions above our own

~ consider ourselves as one church in our city with many expressions rather than remain isolated as many expressions of His church in one city.

{the bottom line}

If I remain isolated thinking only of MY church, then I will not be

~ loving like Jesus loves,

~ thinking of the church like Jesus thinks,

~ involved in the actual work of God, and

~ I will not see "on earth as it is in heaven" in our city.

Do you want to be involved in the work of God? Then beg Him to help you and me think "beyond MY church."

CONSIDER and CONVERSE:

1. Think back on the last three to five comments or thoughts you have had about another local church expression in the city. Were those comments or thoughts laced with encouragement and love and unity or laced with criticism and jealousy and divisiveness?

2. What might I need to repent of and seek forgiveness for in my own life in order to move beyond thinking only of MY church?

3. What might our local church family together need to repent of and seek forgiveness for in order to move beyond thinking only of MY church?

4. Is there any one follower of Jesus or even another entire local church expression that you need to go to and apologize and seek to be reconciled with in order for healing to begin and unity to happen? What could you do to make that happen?

5. What one thing—one next step—will you take to begin to think and live "beyond MY church"?

chapter 1

drop the "MY church" mentality because Jesus' intentions were beyond that

{Imagine Caleb}

Caleb bags groceries. When people go through his line, he has become determined to make them smile, at the least, and to let them know they are loved, as an ideal. Why? Because he is understanding more and more that just "going to church" isn't why Jesus died. He is understanding more that resurrection power in and through his life is not limited to inviting people to "attend church." It's beyond that.

Caleb heard a missionary talk about the importance of what the missionary labeled "church planting." That missionary was speaking, of course, of the adventurous, poverty-stricken, far-off land where he served. The missionary told of the need for new churches where he was and shared story after story of how they were "cultivating the gospel" to see those new churches begin. Caleb was moved. No doubt he should, when he could, go and serve with this missionary. But Caleb had a thought. A Spirit-given thought. That there was not just a need internationally. There was a need right in the sleepy town where he lived and worked and played. He began to wonder, *How can I think and act like a missionary? Maybe new expressions of the church are needed right here. Besides, if I ever did move internationally or even if I stayed right here in the States my whole life, isn't this what Jesus intended for me as His follower? Wouldn't it help to be practicing now?* And he wasn't just thinking about a new Sunday School class within the church family of which he was a part. He was thinking beyond that.

Caleb began dreaming about his family, the neighborhood, the place he worked, the city in which he lived, and the world for which he was burdened. The missionary had shared that over 4 billion people in the world are "lost." He wasn't exactly sure what the missionary classified as lost, but he knew two things for sure. Even if it was a fraction of that number, that was too many. And the sound of anyone not knowing their way in life was haunting to him. He began to imagine what life might be like if he lived to give himself away to his family members, to his neighbors, at work, in the local community, and around the world. What if he not only gave himself away to the people who existed in those spheres of influence? What if he also invited them to join him in giving themselves away with him? That sounded more like "on earth as it is in heaven" to him. This wasn't just a desire to be a more intellectually educated "Christian." He was imagining spirituality beyond himself and his own development.

Reading the story of Jesus a bit differently now, Caleb views Jesus as a Sent One who is now sending him. Thus, he reads the stories with more than just an idea of how he can be a better Christian. He reads them wanting to think more like the Sent One, especially whenever he encounters a friend or a co-worker. He understands that each person he meets matters to Jesus just as much as he has come to understand that he himself matters to Jesus. He wants to follow this Sent One into the everyday of his life and "make disciples." He wants to share His love while learning and living His ways, both with those who already follow Him as well as with those who don't. He doesn't know all that means, but he understands that making disciples is a mandate for him, not just for his pastor or student pastor. He's thinking beyond them.

Caleb listens for the Sent One to prompt him. When he reads the Bible, it allows him to become more and more familiar with the promptings of the Spirit as seen in the Scriptures so that he can then better recognize those promptings in the everyday among the many temptations and desires he feels. Caleb listens for the Sent One to send him with a potentially transformational hug, glance, challenge, or encouragement. He builds friendship minus the agenda of needing to invite them "to church." Rather, he builds friendship with the pure motive of wanting to give away the love that has been so freely given to him by the Sent One, in hopes that others will find their way in Jesus, no matter what church family they end up walking with and no matter who gets the credit.

Thinking and acting like a missionary isn't just some "church growth strategy." He's seeing beyond one expression of the church to the church coming fully alive in the city.

If he is able to make disciples, with the Spirit's help of course, then it is likely that this "church planting" thing might happen through Caleb. He could start new expressions of the church in his home, at work, in the community! He understands that if disciples of Jesus are made, then they will want to live like the Sent One too. They will learn and live His ways and begin to be the church daily too. What if a few of the folks he is learning and living the ways of Jesus with at work start wanting to do that same thing with some of their neighbors? What if he could help them do that? What if from those efforts a new local church expression starts in their neighborhood? He is not worried about the specific form it would take at this point—becoming a 501(c)(3) (whatever that is), calling a pastor, being an "official church" or just being a local ministry of the church in that neighborhood. Regardless, it is being the church.

Caleb is not worried about those silly measurables that he hears people argue over within the church family of which he is a part. He is beginning to believe that the people are the church, and we don't need to get in the way of what the Spirit might be doing in and through His people to see His kingdom come "on earth as it is in heaven." He is not worrying about who gets the credit at all. He sees beyond that to what he must simply be faithful to cultivate daily. For some reason, he believes that the Sent One wants to do something beyond what he could even imagine, and so the outcome (what is reaped) is not as important as the cultivation (what is sowed).

This "Caleb" isn't real, at least not yet. I am prayerful that my son Caleb will have this heart and mentality, but the story of Caleb that launched this chapter is what I imagine God imagines for His followers.

If he were real, then I would likely be telling you about what happened next.

chapter one

That
- ~ his mom began to follow Jesus and began a book club for moms in their neighborhood so they could encourage one another.
- ~ his friend from school began to follow Jesus and started an "I don't know the Bible either but let's read it together" club after school.
- ~ his manager began to follow Jesus after this kid encouraged her with what Jesus taught about love, such that it changed the way she loved her husband and they came back from the brink of divorce.
- ~ his manager, Caleb and a few of their co-workers began to study the Scriptures together and serve weekly at a local soup kitchen.
- ~ some of them got a burden for orphans in the Dominican Republic and began to travel there once a year to love on them and even witnessed three orphans being adopted by families in the US.

All this in that sleepy little town all because Caleb began to think "beyond MY church." And all of these which I described, if they were real, would be new expressions of the church. Not begun by a clergy member, but rather by a 20-something guy who followed Jesus and began to live like the Sent One daily in the city where he lives.

{Imagine what could be in our cities}

This may have been a parable of sorts, but it is happening. It is going on in America and in other parts of the world. It is happening in other parts of the world because there they are experiencing less bottlenecking from the so-called clergy/bureaucracy of denominationalism and more involvement from all followers of Jesus in this continuing movement of God that is seen through His church alive in the everyday.

In America today, there is a big push to start new churches. It's even become a bit trendy and cool. You may have heard it described by the phrase *church planting*. While I am not a fan of that particular descriptor (that's a writing project in the works) and while I do agree that we are seeing some drawn because of the hipness factor being sifted out into very committed leaders and while I do assert that we are seeing some traction when it comes to healthy cultivation for new expressions of His church here in our country, I want to offer one suggestion for the furtherance of this effort in America.

Don't go into the effort with the mindset of starting MY new church in a city thinking you have to have one guy trained in seminary being central to the effort.

Go into the effort with the mindset of involvement from every follower of Jesus and oneness among all the local church expressions in the city. Go into it asking, "How will we cultivate for one new expression while ultimately cultivating for oneness among the many expressions?"

If you don't include this question in the shaping of your dreams and vision for a new expression of the church, then I believe you will be going into the effort without the framework of thinking that Jesus has. Without the mind of Christ in the effort, why in the world would you think the result would honor Him, would be His work, or would even work?

I have been told that my suggestion is too idealistic, too optimistic. Someone even said to me, "Good luck with convincing any pastors with that one." So guess what? I prayed for what to do and this awesome publisher named New Hope Publishers gave me the opportunity to write a book that is intended to get into the hands of every follower of Jesus rather than only attempting to disseminate it through the hands of the clergy. And then maybe we can infect the clergy with security in Christ instead of insecurity as a leader and with the crazy notion of unity around Jesus' mission instead of centralization to one clergy guy's vision.

chapter one

And with regard to how idealistic it is, I know of a church family that was started more than seven years ago that began with a vision of oneness among the local church expressions in the city. They chose as a logo a compass. This certainly was not original to them. It was a pretty popular logo choice over the last ten years. But they chose it with intentionality. They envisioned local church expressions in each of the five compass points of the city uniting together to be the church to their city and beyond. They dreamed instead of just starting one local church expression that maybe there could be more of a regional church expression. Why couldn't the followers of Jesus from the west, north, east, south, and center of the metro area one day unite to be a church of that region together made up of many local expressions but acting as one body to love and serve in the name of Jesus? This new church family believed it to be possible, continues to cultivate for it, and has seen the first fruits of sowing for that kind of unity.

{what Jesus imagined}

I don't think it is far-fetched to say that Jesus doesn't see this idea as a pipe dream or as naive optimism. In fact, He prayed for it (at least in principle) in John 17.

In the same way that you gave me a mission in the world, I give them a mission in the world. I'm consecrating myself for their sakes so they'll be truth-consecrated in their mission. I'm praying not only for them but also for those who will believe in me because of them and their witness about me. The goal is for all of them to become one heart and mind—just as you, Father, are in me and I in you, so they might be one heart and mind with us. Then the world might believe that you, in fact, sent me. The same glory you gave me, I gave them, so they'll be as unified and together as we are— I in them and you in me. Then they'll be mature in this oneness, and give the godless world evidence that you've sent me and loved them in the same way you've loved me.
John 17:18–23 The Message

Jesus is praying in the garden of Gethsemane in this text. I went there in January 2011 with my dad and brother and a group of about 45 folks connected with the New Orleans Seminary. One of my three favorite highlights of the trip was the brief time we spent on the Mount of Olives where that garden is in which Jesus prayed this prayer.

In Jesus' prayer here, He declared that He was giving a mission to His followers just as He was given a mission. The Sent One now sends us.

As the Father has sent me, so I am sending you.
John 20:21 NLT

Exactly what is this mission? Based upon Jesus' commands to His followers, the mission certainly involves loving God and loving one another and loving our neighbor. It is all in an effort to cultivate the gospel that a loving God came near to us and all in hopes that the world would experience "on earth as it is in heaven" together. God has chosen for some crazy reason to trust us, a people with a tendency to divide, instead to live united so that the demonstration of this diverse people unified around a loving God's mission will serve as a living letter of God's love and intention for the humanity He loved and for which Jesus was willing to die. Our mission is to love like He loves so that a people who don't believe they are loved might trust that they are loved and begin to give His love away too.

Short and sweet, as we unite to live sent, people will believe in the One who was sent.

Could it be that simple? Well, hold that thought.

In Jesus' prayer, He next declared that He was being set apart (consecrated) so that His followers could be set apart to be involved in this mission or movement of God. How did He consecrate us? Through His life and death and life again. What this is implying is that anything less than this ideal for which He prayed is less than what He intended through these consecration efforts. So think about it. Do you want to look in His eyes one day and explain that we know He hoped for more but trying to deal with all the disunity and infighting of our one local church was all we could handle. We just couldn't get around to cultivating for "on earth as it is in heaven" in our entire city. Surely He was too optimistic in His consecration efforts.

Let's get blunt for a moment. Do you sincerely think that Jesus hung on a cross with the dream of a redeemed church in His mind that involved isolated, consumer-driven, nonprofit organizations that strategized for more events, hoped for more attendees, budgeted for more facilities, and ignored both the saved and the lost of their city because they had enough problems of their own? Me neither. He clearly hoped for more than that. Are you hoping for more? Do you have the faith and courage to cultivate for it even if it's hard and looked down upon and not received well? I hope so, because that sounds more like what our Savior went through to declare His love. Why wouldn't we go through at least some of that in our efforts to live out His love in our city?

Next, Jesus implied that this mission would result in new followers. He prayed for those who would believe in Him because of the witness of His first followers. Thus, our commitment to being an answer to His prayer would result in new followers and thus new expressions of His church (since His church is simply people following Jesus together).

Then Jesus declared the goal for His followers. He prayed for them "to become one heart and mind" as Jesus had lived in one heart and mind with the Father. In other words, we are to become unified with the Father with regard to the way that He sees the world and people and our life purpose, and then become unified with one another around this mission of declaring the desire of our loving God to be in intimate relationship or oneness with others.

We are to be one heart and mind with the Father as well as with each other if we are going to live as an answer to His prayer in the garden.

John went on to unpack this in First John when he declared throughout that letter that a shared life with God is evidenced by a shared life with others. Our oneness with God is seen in this world by our oneness with each other. And John specified that this is most evidenced by the way we lay our lives down for others (1 John 3:16) and walk in openness and intimacy with one another. Sounds like heaven.

Speaking of heaven, Jesus next prayed words that should grip us to the core. "The same glory you gave me, I gave them, so they'll be as unified and together as we are—I in them and you in me." Reread that, please. Do you think He was serious?

When the Scriptures refer to the glory of God, the implications are always about the revealed presence of God among us—God made known to us—usually only in as much of a manifestation as the people could handle at one time. God revealing His presence to us is something both to be feared as well as to be desired. It's like how some (very strange people in my opinion) want to jump out of a plane. No one approaches that without the fear of what could happen. And yet everyone I have ever spoken to about it declared that it was the most thrilling experience, and they'd do it again.

When Jesus prayed that He was giving the same glory to His followers that was given to Him, He was declaring that in the same way that who God really is was revealed in Him so shall who He really is will be revealed in His followers.

But here's the kicker. Jesus then specifies what that revealed presence would look like AND what the ultimate impact would be. Let's read John 17:23 from *The Message* again:

Then they'll be mature in this oneness, and give the godless world evidence that you've sent me and loved them in the same way you've loved me.

That revealed presence will be demonstrated in the unity of those who call themselves followers of Jesus. And that ultimate impact would thus be the work of God happening in the world. And the implication is then that the work of God will not come alive among you without unity.

Wait a second! You might interrupt here and ask, "Where did He talk about the 'work of God happening' in this?" Well, before I answer your question, let me pose one.

Does the primary description given for your local church expression and for the local church expressions together in the city have anything to do with oneness or unity? If the answer is no, then may I be so bold as to say that the glory of God is not present among you (His revealed presence).

That should bother you. That should disturb you. That should wreck you. Because if His glory is not present, then whose is? If He is not being revealed, then what is?

So back to your presumed question about the work of God. Jesus prayed that we would be mature in unity and that when we were, "*then the world might believe that you, in fact, sent me*" (italics mine). The unity of the followers of Jesus is the validation of His being sent by God. And people believing that God sent Him is the work of God, according to the teaching of Jesus recorded in John 6:29 NASB:

Jesus answered and said to them, "This is the work of God, that you believe in Him whom He has sent."

So, whether we like it or not, the conclusion is that the work of God comes alive among us through our Holy Spirit-enabled unity and not a second before that. His power to unite a selfish, divisive, my agenda-seeking people around a selfless, reconciling, restorative, His kingdom-seeking mission validates to the world the actual divinity and authenticity of the Messiah Jesus.

Now I say "whether we like it or not" because this conclusion should interrupt our "MY church" ventures and scare us to the core that we may have been pursuing our own glory rather than His revealed presence and our own accomplishments rather than His work among us. And if you don't think our unity would validate to the world the authenticity of the Messiah Jesus, then let me ask you this question.

Why then do so many people, from a neighbor on our street to world changers like Gandhi, make statements about their struggle to believe in Jesus because of the actions of His so-called followers?

When I was in Jerusalem, I became friends with Moshe. He is a Jewish learner and teacher who also owns a Jewish art and jewelry shop called A Biblical Shop (www.shorashim.com). If you go there, please tell Moshe I sent you. He told me that he and probably many Jews might consider Jesus to be Messiah if, among other things, His followers lived as one with the Father as Jesus did. We must take his comments and Jesus' prayer seriously.

{the bottom line}

Here's the problem. Not only does a MY church mentality exist among those who are trying to start new expressions of the church, but it also exists all too often among existing local church families. Why?

Is it competition? Pride? Insecurity? Or maybe just that it's all we have known and we supposedly don't know a better or even another way? Whatever is the reason, we must repent of it, beg God for mercy and seek the Spirit's enabling for us as His followers to become the answer to His prayer.

Many expressions of His church are a good thing. Certainly, there are many types of people and many cultures represented in our very diverse humanity. But I would suggest (and I believe Jesus' prayer in the Garden proves it) that Jesus wants His followers involved in those many varied expressions of His church to follow Him with a unity of purpose and mission together. The diversity of humanity becomes beautifully unified when the gospel grips the hearts of people and reconciliation and restoration result.

No more of this MY church stuff. It's not my church. It's not your church. She (the bride) of Christ is His church. If I am using His bride to bring glory to anyone else besides the Groom, then I am most to be pitied.

May we repent and surrender our golden images that we call MY church and MY church vision and MY church building and MY church traditions and MY church programs and MY church growth and beg God for His revealed presence among us through our Spirit-enabled unity. May we unify around His mission in hopes of seeing "on earth as it is in heaven" in our city. May we drop the MY church mentality.

It is not what Jesus intended.

CONSIDER and CONVERSE:

1. Do you think that the ideal of a unified church as a whole in a city is even possible in American church culture? Why or why not?

2. Based on Jesus' prayer in John 17, do you think that unity is what Jesus intended for His followers? What in His prayer supports this belief?

3. Do you agree with this author's conclusion that the work of God will not happen among us in our city without the unity of the followers of Jesus in our city? Why or why not?

4. Do you agree with this author's assertion that the unity of followers of Jesus validates Him being sent as Messiah? Why or why not?

5. What might you and the local church family of which you are a part need to repent of with regard to hindrances to unity?

6. What is the local church family of which you are a part known for in

the community? What has been revealed among you? Pray for God's revealed presence among you.

chapter 2

you matter in His mission, no matter what you think or what the pastor says

We were having lunch at Friday's. It wasn't a Friday, but that's not important. What is important is the question that my friend asked a colleague and me:

"What will be the key to the movement of God happening in Orlando Metro like it is in other parts of the world, second to the primary and obvious answer—the movement of the Holy Spirit?"

Now, since my friend asked that question, please allow me to give two elements of understanding on behalf of my friend who asked it. (1) "Movement of God . . . like it is in other parts of the world" means followers of Jesus making disciples who make disciples who make disciples and so on in such a way that the rapid multiplication of disciples of Jesus occurs. (2) That movement in other parts of the world is characterized by the so-called clergy getting out of the way of what the Spirit is doing and allowing the people of God to join the Spirit in His movement of being the church in the everyday, not just on Sunday.

My colleague answered immediately. He said that the movement depended upon preachers preaching sound doctrine from the pulpit and emphasizing the gospel. While I am all for preaching and sound doctrine and the gospel (I try to preach soundly and gospel-centered every Sunday and often other days of the week), I have to tell you that I disagreed with my friend. Remember, the question was, "What will be the *key*?"

In my opinion, the key to the movement of God happening in our cities will not be about the so-called clergy's response to the movement. The clergy need to be cautious not to bottleneck or get in the way of His movement (I am considered clergy by most, so this is not some disgruntled "church member" here). The clergy furthermore need to be careful not to idealize the Sunday morning preaching event into some ego-driven religious highlight of everyone's week. The clergy ultimately need to be committed to equipping and mobilizing the church as the

Holy Spirit that fills them uses the sound doctrine and beautiful gospel that every follower of Jesus can read in their own copy of the Scriptures. The Holy Spirit can move them to live out how sound that doctrine is and how beautiful that gospel is in the rhythms of their everyday lives and relationships.

The *key* will be the so-called laity, a.k.a. the churchgoer, the pew-sitter, the nonpastoral (and any other label you want to give a misguided, priestlike, improper perspective of the Protestant church effort in America) realizing how essential the Savior has now made them in the ongoing mission of God. The *problem* is that so very often the so-called laity don't realize, believe, or live like they even matter to His mission.

{you matter in His mission . . .}

Please read and then recite and repeat the following statement to yourself every day of your life from here on out as you deny yourself and take up your cross daily and follow Jesus:

I matter in the mission of God.

Say it again. Say it again. Keep repeating it. Now let's process why this could possibly be an accurate declaration.

Three verses about which an entire book has been written (*Live Sent: You Are a Letter*) that need to be highlighted here:

Again he said, "Peace be with you. As the Father has sent me, so I am sending you."
John 20:21 NLT

Clearly, you are a letter from Christ showing the result of our ministry among you. This "letter" is written not with pen and ink, but with the Spirit of the living God. It is carved not on tablets of stone, but on human hearts.
2 Corinthians 3:3 NLT

Truly, truly, I say to you, he who believes in Me, the works that I do, he will do also; and greater works than these he will do; because I go to the Father.
John 14:12 NASB

Did you catch that? God loves us so much that He didn't wait for us to make the first apologetic move to tell Him we were sorry for going our own selfish ways. As such, we became both the beneficiaries of His gospel mission as well as the benefactor of His gospel love. We are now letters from Him sent into our world declaring His near love to a people who are not seeing a near and loving God in the near darkness of their everyday lives. Doesn't that sound like we matter to Him and in His ongoing mission?

And then this "greater works than these" stuff? Was He serious? How could He even say that? How could we ever do greater than He already did? Maybe because He decided before He became Emmanuel that He would fill each of His followers with His Spirit in order to enable them to become Emmanuel's ambassadors into every part of the globe, not just the tiny country of Israel. He decided to make us matter in His mission by declaring us "worth dying for" and then sending us to live a "death-to-self" life for others.

God, who is love, decided to declare us lovely (not by our works but by His), and now He sends us beyond our church buildings out into the world of our everyday to give His love as we live beyond-me and beyond-MY-church lives right smack in the middle of our culture. We didn't declare that we matter in His mission. He declared and intended it that way.

{. . . no matter what you think}

As I suggested in chapter one, it is our unity as His followers around His mission that will take the gospel message to the lost and bring the work of God alive in our cities. And if we believe His mission to be urgent and our unity to be essential and our own everyday lives to be important (because He declared it so), then why aren't we committed to being unified and seeing the work of God come alive in our cities? Could it be because we are too insecure to cultivate for unity and live beyond MY church?

Most people realize that insecurity isolates. But I would suggest that it also divides.

Why? Because when I am consumed with my insecurity, then I am focused only on myself. When I am eaten up with thoughts of what others think about me, then I am not resting in what God thinks about me. When I spend tons of time talking about myself since no one else seems to be talking enough about me, then I am not trusting what the Cross said about me. When I isolate myself out of fear and distrust and past rejections, then I am not giving love like it has been given to me. When I live expecting others to cater to my indulgences and insufficiencies, then I am not putting the interests of others above my own. And if I live out my insecurities in those ways, then what I am really saying with my everyday life is that I don't care about unity and the mission of God and the work of God happening around me. I only care about me. I don't care about anything beyond me. And that does not cultivate for unity. That divides.

Could it be possible that you and I are so insecure and think so much of ourselves that we can't even think of each other? We know that putting the interests of the ones with whom we walk in relationship above our own interests is vital to the life and health of any relationship. So why is it so tough? Why do we let our insecurities plague us so? Whether it's because of paralyzing insecurity or all-consuming arrogance (which is just another way of expressing insecurity), self-absorption is epidemic, even when we don't intend to think only of ourselves.

Like in my marriage. I don't get up any morning of the week and think, "Today I will be selfish. I will hurt my wife with my insensitivity. I even hope she cries." If you get up any morning of the week and think that about anyone, then you need help. Just saying.

Like with my kids. I don't plan my work schedule while thinking, "I am so tired of tucking my kids in bed at night. This trip will be a good break from reading *One Fish. Two Fish. Red Fish. Blue Fish.* for the 1537th time. I want them to know that I don't really care anything about kissing them good night. I have more important pursuits." If you ever think that about your kids or even your neighbor's kids, the ones who picked on your kids and you secretly are hoping that their Capri Sun pouch leaks uncontrollably, then you are sick. Sick I tell you!

Like my brother who lives in northern Tibet (really just Booneville, Mississippi, but northern Tibet sounds much more glamorous). I never approach a week thinking, "I don't want to call him this week. In fact, I don't ever want to call him again. He snorts on the phone a lot and then doesn't pay attention to me like he has four boys running around the house or something." Seriously. If you ever think that about a sibling or friend or even that annoying lady who called to sell you identity protection on your credit card but baits you in by telling you on the voice-mail that she needs to talk to you about your credit card and fraudulent charges, then you have issues.

What am I even saying here? Oh yeah. I am saying that while we all tend toward self-absorption and it is epidemic in our lives evidenced by our actions, we aren't necessarily starting the day hoping to be that way. But when a relationship gets tough or a spouse hurts you or a sibling offends you or a friend's fondness seems to have waned or somebody is trying to make a change to those precious church traditions we are willing to die to preserve, then we typically respond by highlighting our interests that have been offended rather than putting theirs above our own. Why?

Could it be because we don't *live loved*?

Could it be because we don't believe that "God so loved the world"? Jesus taught that we would need to deny ourselves daily to follow Him (Luke 9:23). He also declared that believing that God loves us leads to abundant life in the right now as well as in the not yet (John 3:16).

That's right. John 3:16. The ultimate overused Bible verse. The ultimate football game Bible verse. The ultimate Valentine's Bible verse. Yes, the ultimate life Bible verse. Why?

Because its implications are the most profound.

If you believe that you are loved by the Ultimate Lover, then you will be made to become less and less insecure and selfish day by day and thus be freed to be enabled and empowered to live loved, breath by breath growing in oneness with others, demonstrating your growing oneness with the Father.

When we trust that we are loved, then we can quit living to be loved and rather live to give love. We can grow through our insecurities instead of being paralyzed by them. We can tame our need to highlight ourselves and become more and more genuinely interested in highlighting others.

They won't change overnight, those self-absorbed tendencies. But if we surrender to be cultivated by the One who sowed His love into us, then we can in turn blossom His love (and thus unity) out of our lives—a unity that we could not have reaped on our own. We need the Holy Spirit to blossom this in us and through us. And what would that blossoming look like? Paul asked the same question:

But what happens when we live God's way? He brings gifts into our lives, much the same way that fruit appears in an orchard—things like affection for others, exuberance about life, serenity. We develop a willingness to stick with things, a sense of compassion in the heart, and a conviction that a basic holiness permeates things and people. We find ourselves involved in loyal commitments, not needing to force our way in life, able to marshal and direct our energies wisely. Legalism is helpless in bringing this about; it only gets in the way. Among those who belong to Christ, everything connected with getting our own way and mindlessly responding to what everyone else calls necessities is killed off for good—crucified. Since this is the kind of life we have chosen, the life of the Spirit, let us make sure that we do not just hold it as an idea in our heads or a sentiment in our hearts, but work out its implications in every detail of our lives.

Galatians 5:22–25 The Message

Are you living loved? Do you think you matter in His mission? You do. Believe it and keep believing it. Let His love unify us as His church so that our cities may see how much He loves us as they see our love for one another. You matter in His mission, no matter what you think.

{. . . or what the pastor says}

But what if the pastor is indicating something different? What if the pastor views the Sunday morning proclamation as the most valuable moment in the movement of God each week? What if the pastor expects you to do nothing more than keep inviting people to be amazed by gifted musicians and polished speaking? What if the pastor's actions make it seem like what the pastor does is what really matters in His mission, not what you do?

Or, what if the pastor says that you matter, but then doesn't authenticate that declaration in the vision and programming of the local church family of which you are a part? What if the pastor says that you matter, but then never does anything more than try to convince you of the significance of the pastor's vision and dreams? What if the pastor says that you matter, but then only recruits you to do mindless volunteer stuff that magnifies the Sunday morning event where the pastor is featured?

Does that stuff really happen in the American church?

I really don't think most pastors intend to (wrongly) emphasize all that stuff. But it sure seems to be the default action of the American church to focus primarily on enlisting Sunday morning volunteers rather than equipping and sending disciple-making missionaries into the everyday. No matter what the pastors are saying, their actions all too often are screaming that the laity don't matter in the mission of God.

Speaking of *laity*, I really don't like that term. I am on a quest to come up with a better word or even to eliminate the use of that word in all of church culture. Its history is not a good one, because it indicates the stark contrast of value placement that most people make between the so-called clergy and laity.

I was in Florence, Italy, with my dad. Our city guide was taking us through the Basilica di Santa Maria del Fiore (a.k.a. the Duomo). As we exited the main building of the Duomo, we walked toward an adjacent building connected by a covered walkway. Like many cathedrals of Europe, there were buildings and rooms added for the wealthy and aristocratic of the city over time. This particular building that we were about to walk into was set aside for training and teaching. Above one of the entrances were Latin words that appeared to me, with my expertise from seventh-grade Latin, to indicate a training room for the *laity*. I asked our guide what the words meant. She responded, "Theological Training for the Nonreligious." I asked her if *laity* meant "nonreligious." She said it did, at least in their culture.

Seriously? As though only the clergy are the religious ones. But isn't this how we act in American church culture? While I agree that there is a shift occurring currently, the large majority of the leaders with whom I have discussed the clergy-laity distinction have agreed that for all their tenure in the latter half of the twentieth century, the church of America has seen the "pastor" as central to the church rather than as an equipper of the church. Protestants became catholic again, at least in terms of priesthood. Making disciples as well as making hospital visits became the job of the clergy. Following Jesus for many people became nothing more than church attendance and listening to the pastor preach.

And it seems to me and those same leaders to whom I spoke that the pastors didn't necessarily try to make it so. However, as that trend of clergy being more important occurred, the ego of the pastors began to crave this affirmation and centrality, as such, that they did emphasize the gathering of the church far above the sending of the church. And thus, the nonreligious emerged in the local church expressions of America.

Pure and undefiled religion in the sight of our God and Father is this: to visit orphans and widows in their distress, and to keep oneself unstained by the world.
James 1:27 NASB

If that's what it means to God to be religious, then we certainly became nonreligious in the latter half of the twentieth century in the American church, when more money and time went into building and maintaining more attractive gathering spaces than went into helping the broken and poor. And according to Amos 4 and 5, there's blood on our hands to show for it and accountability to come.

Again, I do agree that there is a shift occurring. A revolution of sorts. A reFUNCTIONation, as I like to call it, rather than a reFORMation. The function of following Jesus, loving God and one another and the orphan and widow, is being renewed. I am witnessing it and hope you are too. And it is a breath of fresh air in light of what has been.

So, I challenge you as the so-called laity to quit distinguishing between the clergy and the laity so much. In fact, please email me your ideas for new terms (invitingconversation@gmail.com). The ones we call clergy would probably better be called *equippers* according to the New Testament. And the ones we call laity would probably better be called *followers* or *saints* or *priests* or *kings* or *forgiven sinners now on mission*.

The bottom line is that the nonclergy matter just as much, if not more, in the everyday mission of God. You matter in the mission of God, no matter what you think or what the pastor says.

Why? Because Jesus said so and the Bible tells me so, first and foremost. But also for this very significant reason:

The person who is living to "equip" you for the daily ministry of the gospel does not live with your spouse or sibling, does not live beside your neighbor, does not recreate with your friend, does not work next to your co-worker, cannot always serve the local community at the time that fits into your schedule, and cannot always go when you can go across the world.

One person cannot go demonstrate "God with us" (Emmanuel) the way that many people can. That's why Jesus said His followers would do greater things than He did. Because we have more hands and feet and ears and mouths and hearts that can be used by a loving God longing to express His near love to a hurting people.

Does that last sentence in any way describe your everyday? If not, then you may be misguided with regard to your value in His mission and you may be misunderstanding the very reason you have been asked to follow Jesus.

Go matter to others, because He intended for you to matter in His mission.

CONSIDER and CONVERSE:

1. What will be the key to the movement of God happening in the city where you live, second to the primary and obvious answer—the movement of the Holy Spirit?

2. What are some better labels or categories that you can think of besides clergy and laity? Does there need to be a distinction? Why or why not?

3. What are some of the insecurities and fears that plague followers of

Jesus and hinder them from really participating in the mission of God in the daily?

4. Does your equipper both talk and walk like you matter? If not, pray about kindly discussing it with your equipper. If so, thank your equipper for serving and equipping you according to the ways of the New Testament rather than the ways of twentieth-century culture.

5. What are some ways you can begin or continue to matter together in the city where you live? When will you go matter? Please share any stories with me (invitingconversation@gmail.com).

chapter 2b

you don't matter as much as you sometimes think, though

I grew up in New Orleans. The building in which our church family gathered had to be bulldozed after Hurricane Katrina. So did many of the homes and apartments and communities where we served and ministered and befriended. It's still a bit surreal not to have existing locations of many of those childhood memories to visit.

One memory I have, though, I wish I could forget. As I am sure you can imagine, many groups came from out of town into New Orleans to serve in the inner city. They came typically with a sense of call. They came typically with a craving to serve (and a craving for some of the great New Orleans food). They came typically with an idea already in mind as to the grand difference they could make in our town. And they came having to overcome perceptions already held by the people they were going to serve and change and transform.

Reread that last paragraph and think about this question—how many of those groups came to town to ask our names and ask what we might need before they assumed they knew?

I call this the "superior syndrome." Many "Christians" and church groups are infected by it. I am convinced it must be some virus that exists inside of "fellowship halls" in which the groups plan their service projects and missions trips. Or it must be some bug that lives inside of 15-passenger vans and bites all riders as they journey toward their service locations.

Seriously, if you have ever walked into a service situation thinking more about how good it was for you to be there than about how good it was to meet and become friends with someone you would encounter there, then you may have superior syndrome. If you have ever gone on a missions trip with every detail preplanned and expectations already in order about the number of names you would write inside of your Bible to add to the list of the people that you have personally transformed with your presence, then you may have superior syndrome. If you have been excited about serving one day for a few hours but unwilling to become friends for many days over many hours, then you may have superior syndrome.

{the church tends to be arrogant}

The church tends to think of ourselves as the good ones now trying to help the bad ones.

Simply put, this kind of thinking is arrogant. It's like we forget that grace both saved us and sustains us. We trusted in the gracious love given at the Cross, but now look at us. We have done so much since. We are so good and accomplished and only have a little debt left on that building, so now we can go do a few good community service projects and make a difference. We have all the latest ideas and notions. Pay no mind to the fact that most of them are Christianized versions of corporate ideas and cultural norms. We put a fish symbol on them, so now they are especially good. People need us. They need us or they won't see Jesus.

We may have it backwards.

In Matthew 25:31–46 (NASB), Jesus spoke of separating the goats and the sheep. He said in verses 34 to 36 of the sheep [His followers]:

Then the King will say to those on His right, "Come, you who are blessed of My Father, inherit the kingdom prepared for you from the foundation of the world. For I was hungry, and you gave Me something to eat; I was thirsty, and you gave Me something to drink; I was a stranger, and you invited Me in; naked, and you clothed Me; I was sick, and you visited Me; I was in prison, and you came to Me."

Notice how they reacted in verses 37 to 39:

Then the righteous will answer Him, "Lord, when did we see You hungry, and feed You, or thirsty, and give You something to drink? And when did we see You a stranger, and invite You in, or naked, and clothe You? When did we see You sick, or in prison, and come to You?"

Jesus said in verses 41 to 43 of the goats:

Then He will also say to those on His left, "Depart from Me, accursed ones, into the eternal fire which has been prepared for the devil and his angels; for I was hungry, and you gave Me nothing to eat; I was thirsty, and you gave Me nothing to drink; I was a stranger, and you did not invite Me in; naked, and you did not clothe Me; sick, and in prison, and you did not visit Me."

Notice how they reacted in verse 44:

Then they themselves also will answer, "Lord, when did we see You hungry, or thirsty, or a stranger, or naked, or sick, or in prison, and did not take care of You?"

Isn't it obvious that the "sheep" thought more about those they served rather than thinking so highly of their own acts of service? They would have been willing to keep serving regardless of the return on investment. And isn't it clear that the "goats" were keeping score, expecting their acts of service to be noticed? This kind of thinking makes us less likely to keep serving unless we are praised as a good person who serves well. The problem with this kind of thinking is that most opportunities to give unconditional love are not met with unconditional love in return. So will we stop giving love unless we receive it? Jesus said that anyone can do that (Matthew 5:46–47). Anyone can keep score, but not just anyone can keep serving when the score doesn't matter. But be careful that you don't start keeping score of the fact that you don't keep score. It's a fine line, isn't it?

Maybe it wouldn't be such a selfish/selfless tension if we would take the focus completely off ourselves and off what others see in us. Maybe it wouldn't be such a hard balance if we would quit thinking about others noticing us and quit thinking about others being changed by us—if we would instead simply think about Jesus. What if we just fixed our thoughts and eyes on Him?

Look back at that Matthew 25 teaching. I didn't mention how the King responded to the questions of the sheep and the goats. Check this out:

[To the sheep verse 40] *The King will answer and say to them, "Truly I say to you, to the extent that you did it to one of these brothers of Mine, even the least of them, you did it to Me."*

[To the goats verse 45] *Then He will answer them, "Truly I say to you, to the extent that you did not do it to one of the least of these, you did not do it to Me."*

Maybe we are too concerned about people seeing Jesus in us. You might say, "What?! I thought you just wrote a chapter about how much people seeing Jesus in each of us daily matters!" I did. But when "people seeing Jesus in us" becomes "people seeing how good I am," then that fine line of focus between mission and myself has been crossed. People seeing Jesus in me and me thinking about how much people are seeing Jesus in me are two very different things.

If I am reading this story correctly, then there is more to draw from it than just keeping score and not keeping score and just ignoring the poor and serving the poor lessons. If I am reading this story correctly, then a very significant lesson from Jesus' teaching here is this:

I need to focus less on people seeing Jesus in me and more on seeing Jesus in people.

So if everyone I meet could fall into the category of "one of these brothers of mine," as Jesus called them in Matthew 25, and if serving "one of these brothers of mine" also means I am serving Jesus ("you did it to Me"), then doesn't that imply that I am serving Jesus when I serve anyone? And if I take this seriously, then doesn't this way of thinking mean that when I look into the eyes of my spouse, my friend, my co-worker, the poor, the lonely, the orphan, the widow… anyone, then God is giving me the chance to look into His eyes? How could this be?

Maybe God intended it as such, since He is love and would obviously show up any time love is given.

When I look into the eyes of a hungry or thirsty or unknown or naked or sick or imprisoned person, then I am, in that moment, being given the opportunity by God to look into His eyes and see more clearly than at any other moment "on earth as it is in heaven." Then I am living most how God intended me to live, and thus I am able to see His presence more than at any other time. Even more than on Sunday morning when the preacher is preaching (read the last chapter if you missed it).

{let's pray and repent}

If this is the case and, just to amuse me, let's assume that it is, then pray about these possibilities for your daily life and for the life of the church as a whole in the city where you live:

:: *Lord, please help me to be open to being transformed by You while serving (especially more than I am thinking about someone being transformed by my service).*

:: *Lord, please help us to quit expecting our city to "come to church," and instead help us as followers of Jesus to go and "be the church" together to our city.*

:: *Lord, please awaken our local church expression and the church as a whole in our city to think beyond the numbers of people coming to MY church programs* increasing, *and instead think of the number of divorces and suicides and addictions and domestic violence cases and consequences of selfishness in our city* decreasing *because we live out Your gospel in our city beyond the walls of our church building.*

:: *Lord, please help us not to think so highly of ourselves that we assume what the people around us need. Please give us wisdom through relationship as we learn names and ask our city the question, "What do you need?"*

CONSIDER and CONVERSE:

{Just a point of clarity—when I write "the church" in these questions, I am speaking of not just one local church expression, but rather of all of the followers of Jesus being the church together to their city.}

1. Do you have superior syndrome? If so, how can you be cured of it?

2. Is the church open to being transformed while serving, more than transforming someone being served?

3. Does the church think so much of themselves that their city should obviously come to visit them, or do they think so much of their city that the church should obviously go to visit them?

4. Does the church focus only on the numbers that flock to their various programs, or does the church focus on the city "numbers" (statistics) that indicate real issues and real change?

5. Does the church think so highly of what they can do for their city that they don't even ask their city what they need, or does the city think so highly of what the church does for them that they think of the church first when they have a need?

chapter 3

am I addicted to MY church?

They say the first step to overcoming addiction is admitting the problem. So, ask yourself this question—am I addicted to MY church?

You declare, "No way! I am committed to the kingdom of God!" Consider these questions that may reveal otherwise:

::   *the last time you left a Sunday morning worship gathering, was your comment: (a) The preacher just didn't come with the A game today. I didn't get anything out of it, or (b) What a privilege that followers can gather together as a family. Who do I know that might need to know such a loving family exists?*

::   *the last time you were evaluating local church expressions or "shopping for a new church" as they say, was your comment: (a) I don't see anything there that really appeals to me and my family, or (b) Is this a local church expression with whom we could give ourselves away as a family?*

::   *the last time you even processed what "success" would mean for the local church expression of which you are a part, did your prayer go something like: (a) Lord, please send us more people that we may grow, or (b) Lord, please send us as Your people into our city that they may know You and that they may grow?*

::   *the last time you considered why the local church expression of which you are a part even exists, was your answer: (a) We exist to be a place where people can come to connect with God, or (b) We exist to be a people who take the love of God near to the people of our city so that they can connect with God?*

::   *the last time you thought about what "revival" would even look like in the city where you live, did you imagine: (a) "MY church" would get "on fire" for God, or (b) the people of our city would see HIS church unified in love and purpose, not caring about whose local church expression benefited?*

If you answered (a) to any of those questions, then you may be "addicted to MY church." If you answered (a) to any of those questions, but you still don't think you are addicted, because what's so bad about wanting to get something out of MY church for me anyway, then you may be, as they say "in denial."

{what I get versus what I give}

Here's the common issue—people tend to approach "church" thinking about what they get out of church rather than thinking about what they get to give as the church.

People have told me something like, "But, Jason. Come on, man. It's OK for me to get something for myself out of church. Otherwise how would I be able to give something?"

Let me ask you two questions:

1. What more are you expecting to get than a love relationship with Jesus Christ daily?
2. When do you think you will "get" the most out of church—when you are focused on getting or giving?

I am not saying that you and I don't need to grow in Christ or study His Word or walk in a small group or connect our kids with a discipling kids ministry or serve locally and globally together. I am not saying that we don't need to look for those things when evaluating what local church expression with which we will connect. I am just saying that those things are not for personal spiritual development only. They must be catalysts for living sent daily to give the love I have been given away. They must be relational elements of who I am and whose I am and who I am being made to be in Christ.

If I focus only on my growth in Christ, then I am missing the intent of the One whom I say I follow. If I focus only on studying His Word, then I am hoarding a treasure that transforms daily living. If I focus only on connecting in a small group, then I miss the opportunity to love a lost neighbor who needs that small group as much as I do. If I focus only on finding a good children or student ministry, then I am potentially cultivating into my kids the mindset that "church" is for their enjoyment, and I am most likely also skirting the responsibility of being the primary teacher and mentor to my kids, expecting the church to provide what God intended for me to give. If I am only looking for my niche in which to serve, then I am more focused on serving my obligation-to-serve fetish rather than focusing on the people whom I am serving.

I had one leader tell me, "Jason, you are totally missing the need to care for the "sheep" here. It can't only be about living sent and caring for the lost and thinking beyond ourselves."

I honestly feel that this kind of thinking is a gross misunderstanding of the new commandment Jesus gave His followers in the first century (and ultimately to us as His followers today) found in John 13:34–35.

A new commandment I give to you, that you love one another, even as I have loved you, that you also love one another. By this all men will know that you are My disciples, if you have love for one another.
John 13:34–35 NASB

How do we miss that what Jesus is saying here is that it is our love for one another as His followers that both authenticates and enables others to see the ways of Jesus lived out among them? All men will know that you

chapter three

are My disciples = others will see you living like you know Me and living out my ways on earth as it is in heaven. In other words, without caring for one another, for the "sheep" as that leader told me, we cannot live out the mission God intended for His church. If caring for the "sheep" doesn't lead to being sheep as Jesus intended us to be, then we are not really caring for the "sheep." We are just caring about how many sheep stick around. And if we worry so much about taking care of ourselves, then we won't take care of one another or the hurting and broken and overlooked around us. Thus His work won't be done, especially because His work won't be done without our love for one another as His followers.

And not just love for the followers in "MY church," but love among all the followers of our city. But we will get to that in a minute. Let's finish this thought.

The problem in the thinking that we can give so much that "our own" don't get enough is that we are not applying the very teachings of God Himself. Read Isaiah 58:6–11 (NASB). This is God talking through His prophet Isaiah:

Is this not the fast which I choose, to loosen the bonds of wickedness, to undo the bands of the yoke, and to let the oppressed go free and break every yoke? Is it not to divide your bread with the hungry and bring the homeless poor into the house; when you see the naked, to cover him; and not to hide yourself from your own flesh? "Then your light will break out like the dawn, and your recovery will speedily spring forth; and your righteousness will go before you; the glory of the LORD will be your rear guard. Then you will call, and the LORD will answer; you will cry, and He will say, "Here I am." If you remove the yoke from your midst, the pointing of the finger and speaking wickedness, and if you give yourself to the hungry and satisfy the desire of the afflicted, then your light will rise in darkness and your gloom will become like midday. And the LORD will continually guide you, and satisfy your desire in scorched places, and give strength to your bones; and you will be like a watered garden, and like a spring of water whose waters do not fail.
Isaiah 58:6–11 NASB

We must quit saying we trust God to take care of our every need, but then live as His church like He won't do what He says. We must quit focusing on preserving MY church and on getting mine. When we do this, we are basically telling God that we don't believe what He said in Isaiah 58. We must believe that when we give ourselves for the oppressed both within our church family ("your own flesh") and within our city that we will not lack for what it will take to keep giving. In fact, it is only when we do give generously, as our heavenly Father has given to us, that we will see God "continually guide" us and that our "light will rise in darkness" and that our flow of generosity will continue to flow like a never-ending stream.

Jesus taught this same principle.

If your first concern is to look after yourself, you'll never find yourself. But if you forget about yourself and look to me, you'll find both yourself and me. . . . Give a cool cup of water to someone who is thirsty, for instance. The smallest act of giving or receiving makes you a true apprentice. You won't lose out on a thing.
Matthew 10:39,42 The Message

Isn't it clear? If you or I have as our first concern to look after self and if any local church expression has as first concern to look after self (what we get vs. what we give), then we will never be neither what we want to be nor what Jesus intended us to be. But if we forget about self and give as Jesus leads and like Jesus gave, then we "won't lose out on a thing."

Wait a second.

May we take seriously what Jesus said. A focus on "MY church" and what I get out of church will result in nothing that He wants. A focus on being HIS church daily, even in the smallest act of giving some small cup of His living water to the thirstiest of souls, will result in exactly what He intended for His church and more than what we could have imagined as His church.

Before we move on from that point, please, please, please, please take it in. Commit to process it. Commit to dialogue about it with the local church family of which you are a part. Ask one another—are we only looking out for what we get out of church, or are we looking ultimately for what we give as His church?

{revival or obedience?}

And this leads us to the point—in order for our city to see God the way God wants our city to see Him, His church must live as God intended His church to live. He intended us to be less concerned about the preservation of MY church and more concerned about the generosity of His church overall. He wants us to quit acting like we are the only good church thing going on in town and everybody ought to come, and instead herald all the good He is doing among all of His followers in our city and go daily together to be His church. He wants all of us as His followers, loving one another and living on mission daily in unity, to go give His love away into the people of our city.

Remember we have already examined the fact that, according to what Jesus prayed in John 17, the maturity of unity among His followers will be what most reveals the presence of God in our communities and thus most allows for the work of God to come alive in our cities. If this is the case, then why don't we think and act "beyond MY church"? Why don't we live as though it would be OK for another local expression of His church to be "more successful" than our own? Why do we pray for the work of God to happen among us, but then we don't live out obediently what He already prayed for us?

Am I crazy for thinking this is so significant, or do you agree that our disregard for unity among followers and our disobedience to what Jesus prayed for us is a very serious issue?

Does anyone else find it strange that local church expressions commit to pray for revival in our cities, asking God to awaken people to know and follow Him, and yet those same local church expressions rarely commit to pray for unity among the followers of Jesus in our cities? Shouldn't we be asking God to awaken us and change us to live out His love and mission together, living obediently in unity so that the people of our city might witness the near love of God through our selfless "sentness" and thus believe in the One who sent us?

Does anyone else worry that our desire for revival may be driven by a selfish craving for another great religious experience with God rather than driven by a selfless hunger to see others experience His near love and be transformed themselves?

I suggest this is our current reality in the "American church" because of the desire for revival over unity and the lack of obedience to what Jesus prayed for us. Isn't it totally irrational to think that God would bring "revival" among a people who are showing, for the most part, complete disregard for what He Himself prayed for His people?

We do need revival, but not for another emotional high or religious fix. We need revival to come alive to the significance of unity among every local expression of His church in a city so that those followers can be the church to the people of that city. We do need revival, but not for an explosion of growth in MY church. We need revival for the sake of the lost being found and those who do not believe in the love of a near God to believe that He loves them.

And according to what Jesus prayed, this will happen when—and only when—His followers take seriously His prayer for unity and are obedient to take His love near to the people of our cities in unified fashion. When we do, He will show Himself and people will be most likely to believe in the One who was sent and who now sends us.

I believe that if you don't even think about unity among the followers of Jesus in the city where you live, then you don't really care about God's revealed presence in the city where you live.

Instead of praying for revival, may we live out what Jesus prayed. Instead of praying for awakening, may we wake daily to live what He has already commanded.

{ what has led to this addiction?}

What could have led to this addiction with which we tend to struggle? What is really the issue that keeps me stagnant and often spiraling in this all-consuming craving for the next religious emotional fix?

Like most addictions, this one ravages both those of us who are addicted as well as all the loved ones surrounding us. But, there is not just one family or one extended family affected here. It is the "family of God." No wonder God Himself would offer the remedy, coming Himself to free us from our addiction to self. But we keep playing with fire, only this time instead of the seemingly bad stuff it's the good stuff of the work of MY church or my personal spiritual development. All the while, though, the "family of God" is ravaged by the self-absorbed tendencies of those who call themselves members of His family, simply because we fail to live beyond self and beyond MY church and take togetherness and sentness as seriously as Jesus did when He prayed for it in the Garden of Gethsemane.

Why? May I offer three suggestions as to what possibly may be keeping us trapped in this addiction? Could it be that we value certain things over others, specifically certain things that God does not value in the same way? Consider what may be keeping us addicted—a value system that doesn't match up with the value system of Jesus.

1) entity over evidence

In church culture today, particularly in Europe and America, we tend to focus on the entity of one "church on a corner" over the evidence of *the* church in our city. This is not biblical.

One of the men who mentored me, Bill Faulkner, said it well as we sipped coffee together one day. "The New Testament does not speak of the church in the way that we do in America. We speak of our respective churches across the city. The New Testament spoke of one church alive in a city." I had already been noticing this, but Bill's assertion made me dig deeper. What I found astounded me.

The New Testament does not seem to focus on any one entity of church. Rather, the Scriptures highlight the evidence of the church alive together in a city.

There is no First John the Baptist of Jerusalem. There is no Second Apollos Community Church in Corinth. In fact, there is "the Church of Ephesus" and "the Church of Antioch" and the like, but that in no way implies that these were respective entities competing for the people of those cities. Rather they were, at least in ideal form, references to the evidence of the church alive and unified on mission in those cities in various expressions within families, neighborhoods, and markets.

There is no 501(c)(3) to be filed or nonprofit status to achieve. I understand that in modern context there may be occasions where nonprofit status could be significant. But the important thing is not creating 501(c)(3)s that have to be preserved and maintained rather than being neighbors together and completely generous together and free to give it all away if we feel led to do so. That need to maintain our entities seems to be preventing us from demonstrating the evidence of the church in our cities.

That drive to be the most attractive and successful entity in town prevents us from demonstrating the evidence of the church in our cities too.

Paul addressed this sort of competition that leads to divisiveness in his first letter to Corinth:

I have a serious concern to bring up with you, my friends, using the authority of Jesus, our Master. I'll put it as urgently as I can: You must get along with each other. You must learn to be considerate of one another, cultivating a life in common. I bring this up because some from Chloe's family brought a most disturbing report

to my attention—that you're fighting among yourselves! I'll tell you exactly what I was told: You're all picking sides, going around saying, "I'm on Paul's side," or "I'm for Apollos," or "Peter is my man," or "I'm in the Messiah group." I ask you, "Has the Messiah been chopped up in little pieces so we can each have a relic all our own? Was Paul crucified for you? Was a single one of you baptized in Paul's name?"
1 Corinthians 1:10-13 The Message

Paul went on in the entirety of 1 Corinthians 3 to challenge them toward union in Christ and thus a demonstration of the evidence of the God who is at work in and through them. Check it out for yourself.

Pastor Dave Gibbons of Newsong Community Church spoke at Radicalis, a four-day conference at Saddleback Church in Southern California. I was not privileged to attend, but I came across an article published by www.theChristianPost.com about what Gibbons spoke on just as I was writing this book (talk about good timing).

Gibbons questioned whether Christians really consider one another "brothers and sisters." He said, "The reason why the world looks at us and says 'sham' is because we preach 'brothers and sisters,' 'family,' and 'unity' stuff and we actually don't live it." He then called on pastors to collaborate as opposed to "doing your own thing." He spoke of collaboration not just in terms of a once-a-year joint initiative, but on every level. "What would happen," he posed, "if all the churches were to forgo their individual names and just simply called themselves 'the church?' You can do a lot for the kingdom of God if you forget about your brand."

My friend Kennan used to be the national marketing director for Red Lobster. My kids like their "Warm Chocolate Chip Lava Cookie," but that's not really important right now. What is important is that when Kennan left Red Lobster after about 20 years, he started a business called Brand Catalyst. He is really good at getting businesses to understand the importance of branding and, even more than that, being consistent in their branding and marketing emphases so that the marketed brand matches the delivered brand.

Two thoughts here. One is that what Kennan leads companies to do—be who they promote themselves to be—maybe the church needs to do. Like Gibbons asserted, we talk "family of God" but we don't live it out. The second thought is really a question—does the church need any other "brand" besides Jesus?

If any local expression of the church is promoting their own creatively designed brand more than they are promoting God's own creatively designed brand (His Son), then hasn't that local expression of the church become nothing more than a nonprofit entity that seeks to promote itself in the same way that a business promotes itself?

Is that what we've become? An entity that needs to be promoted? An entity that needs to sharpen its brand (Jesus needs sharpening, right)? An entity that has to meet a bottom line? A business?

Rick Warren said it well via Twitter: "Jesus began His church as a FAMILY. It changed to an institution in Rome, a political view in Europe, and then a business in America."

Ouch! Let's get honest, real honest here. You and the leadership team of the local church expression of which you are a part: do you all set vision and strategy more focused on your own entity of church on your own street corner or for the sake of "planting and watering" for the evidence of the church to blossom in the city where you live?

Entity-over-evidence kind of thinking and living is a reason why we stay addicted to and don't live beyond MY church.

2) personal development over community demonstration

A leader told me that their leadership team was too busy focusing on taking their own church to the next level to worry about what all the

chapter three

other churches in the area were doing. My heart broke. I have to believe that Jesus' heart ached over his statement too.

Let me ask you what may seem to be an unrelated question. And let me give a disclaimer. I assure you that I can demonstrate with many, many references in the Scriptures that what I am about to rhetorically propose is biblical on all counts. But if you don't believe me, then please go search it out yourself. So here's the question:

Is spiritual maturity measured with a mirror or with community?

Thinking back again to John 17, Jesus referred to the unity for which He was praying as "maturity." That "maturity" was demonstrated not via personal introspection, but rather through the evidence of love and unity among a community of believers.

Why is it that both on a personal level as well as on a local church expression level we measure what we suppose to be spiritual maturity with a mirror rather than with loving relationships?

We have already examined, earlier in this chapter, how significant this was to Jesus in the new command that He gave. He went so far as to assert that others would know that we are learning and living His ways through our love for one another. In no way at all is that a reference to looking myself in the mirror and seeing if I have loved well. Whether I have loved well can only be seen in the context of community.

John expounded on Jesus' teachings in his first letter (1 John) when, as my own summary to that letter, he would assert that a shared life with God (what would seem to be another way to say spiritual maturity) is seen most in a shared life with others.

Jesus even hung all of the other commands on this same premise (Matthew 22:40). All of God's commands are summed up in and lived out through our love for God and for one another. However, our seemingly misunderstanding what really matters to God has led us to understand spiritual maturity in a nonbiblical way.

I have asked people many times in Q and A sessions to tell me what they think are indicators of spiritual maturity. All of the answers dealt with elements of personal development, like knowing Scripture and "church attendance" and going on a missions trip. Those are by no means bad things, but they are not the real indicator of spiritual maturity. I know folks who do all three and yet are so unkind and unloving, rarely placing the interests of others above their own. That's not spiritually mature. That's just personal religious development.

It's like we think God went to the trouble to put on skin and make amends for our betrayal before we even said we were sorry all so that we could personally live some individualistically fulfilled religious lifestyle. All so that we could be "good" for God. How could this be so when God-in-skin Himself avoided the compliment "good" (Luke 18:19)? Could it be because God did not go to all that gracious, loving trouble so that we could hold a mirror up to ourselves and feel good about our performances for Him?

This not only applies to our own personal development, but also to our local church expression development too. The "MY church" mentality leads us toward mirror-type evaluating and mirror-type comparisons as respective local church expressions, and it hinders us from living with the kind of unity that would demonstrate spiritual maturity and exemplify the kind of loving Father who is shaping us into a beautiful "on earth as it is in heaven" community of transformed, previously self-addicted people.

When we decide to conduct ourselves like the interests of other local church expressions matter more than our own interests, then maybe this spiritual maturity we all strive for will show itself. But as long as we continue to value personal development over community demonstration, we will stay addicted to and not live beyond MY church.

3) my satisfaction over city transformation

A lot has been made in the last several years over the fact that consumerism is plaguing church culture. It does seem to be true, especially when church leaders strategize to attract more people to their programs than they strategize to send people to love their spouse and neighbor and co-worker. It seems that church leaders have swallowed hook, line, and sinker the notion that if we don't satisfy the consumer, then the consumer won't come. The problem with this is that we have made "church" into a product rather than a people. I am most certain that this grieves God.

Wikipedia has a fascinating article on "consumerism" found at this Web address: http://en.m.wikipedia.org/wiki/Consumerism. An excerpt from that article reads:

"Consumerism is a social and economic order that is based on the systematic creation and fostering of a desire to purchase goods and services in ever greater amounts. . . . In economics, consumerism refers to economic policies placing emphasis on consumption. In an abstract sense, it is the belief that the free choice of consumers should dictate the economic structure of a society . . . in this article the term 'consumerism' refers to the sense first used in 1960, 'emphasis on or preoccupation with the acquisition of consumer goods' (Oxford English Dictionary)."

Is it just me, or does that sound eerily like a church growth seminar taught to take the local expression of which you are a part "level"? "Fostering of a desire to purchase goods and services in ever greater amounts" sounds a lot like what local church expressions do every Sunday morning. We try to make the performance so good that it will keep consumers coming back for more. So good that we will create "policies placing emphasis on consumption" that in turn consume church leaders' time and energy, so much so that they bring leftovers home day after day and week after week. The problem comes when those church leaders begin to think and act like "the free choice of consumers should dictate" the structure of their church society even more than the mandates of the One who started this "company" in the first place. In turn, due in large part to the fact that these church leaders let this consuming trend continue, people expect more and more in this "preoccupation with the acquisition of consumer goods," otherwise known as "church."

My heart hurts badly even typing out that last paragraph. I recently had a local church leader in our city tell me how fatigued he is and how much his family is suffering because of the event-driven and consumer-driven way that the local church expression of which he is a part "conducts their business."

We are fostering a mentality that drives people to be either satisfied with "church" and stick around or be unsatisfied and find a new product that satisfies.

I would suggest that this is sinful (absolutely self-absorbed) for two reasons:

1. because approaching "church" like a product to be consumed completely devours any compulsion to engage in and stick with and grow through the good and bad of loving relationships both with other followers of Jesus as well as with those who Jesus referred to as "lost."
2. because loving the people of our city and meeting the needs of the people in our city gets ignored while we look for the next church product that will satisfy.

Shouldn't the gospel being lived out and lived near and lived among the people of our cities be priority to the church? The age-old question comes to mind again—if the local expression of the church of which you are a part suddenly vanished from the community where you live, would anyone even notice? And if they noticed, would it be because a building sat vacant or because people they considered to be friends had disappeared?

I go to the movies a lot. I get popcorn and a cola, interacting with the workers there. The turnover ratio for the employees there is high, so most don't know me. They just want me to swipe my card and help Hollywood and the local owner of that theater make another buck. I am nothing more than a consumer there. They would not miss me if I never came back or if I just went to another theater.

If the same is true with regard to how the people of a particular city know or don't know the local church expressions of that city, then I would suggest that the local church expressions in that city are nothing more than consumers of the church. They are not being the church, they are just "going to church." They are not living sent; rather they are just looking for the next great product to be presented.

They value their own satisfaction over the transformative work of the gospel alive among the people of that city. Thus, they will remain addicted to and not live beyond MY church.

{am I addicted to MY church?}

Here's what's so very sad. It's the consequences of this MY church addiction.

Disunity among followers. Self-absorbed programming that benefits me rather than selfless mission that God uses to transform a city. Unreconciled relationships among so-called members of the "family of God." Church splits instead of church starts. Church infighting instead of church influencing. Church sterility instead of church fruitfulness. And we wonder why the gospel doesn't seem to be having an effect in our community.

Jesus prayed for unity among His followers. He prayed that we would think and act beyond MY church. Why? So that in our love and unity and commitment to give ourselves away, *the world would know* and believe in the One who was sent, who showed God's love in how He gave Himself away.

Am I addicted to MY church? Or will I admit I have a problem, repent of thinking like an addicted consumer, confess to living in denial, and surrender so that I can begin to think and act as Jesus intended His church to think and act?

May we follow Jesus alongside one another in our cities, committed to planting and watering the gospel together into the lives of the people of our cities in hopes that "on earth as it is in heaven" will blossom in our cities. Then, and only then, will the church move beyond MY entity toward the evidence of Him.

CONSIDER and CONVERSE:

1. Am I addicted to MY church? Who could I admit this to and possibly begin to journey with toward thinking and living beyond MY church?

2. Do I think more about what I get out of church rather than what I give as the church? What are some practical steps toward making that different? HINT: Praying for Jesus to help is the first one.

3. Is there a local church expression in the city where I live that's thinking and living in such a way that people who live here would see more than just individual entities of "church" existing in the city? What might the local church expression of which I am a part have to change in order for there to at least be one?

4. When I think about wanting to be "spiritually mature," what are the first three to five things that come to mind? Are any of them indicative that I think of more than just personal development?

5. Does the local church expression of which I am a part exist to get

bigger or to see our city transformed? Whatever the answer, why am I giving that particular answer?

6. PRAY. Jesus, help me to be satisfied fully in You and in thinking and living with You and like You—fully beyond self and completely for the sake of our loving Father being made known.

chapter 4

am I cultivating for "on earth as it is in heaven" in our city or just trying to add members to MY church?

M ay I ask you a question? I guess you have no choice if you keep reading.

What would "on earth as it is in heaven" look like if you saw it in the city where you live?

Jesus prayed in Matthew 6:10 that God's "will be done, on earth as it is in heaven."

Do you think He really meant that? The stuff of heaven happening here among the stuff of earth? Is that even possible?

With all of the pain and tragedy and difficulty and betrayal and deceit and oppression going on in this world, could the church be naive enough to think that "on earth as it is in heaven" could even happen? May I suggest to you that whether believing that notion to be possible is naive or not:

> *The church must hope for and pray for "on earth as it is in heaven," simply because the one who is the head of the church hoped for and prayed for "on earth as it is in heaven."*

And if we do not, then how can we say we follow the Head of our church?

Consider it this way instead—with all the pain and tragedy and difficulty and betrayal and deceit and oppression going on in this world, what else would the church hope and pray for but "on earth as it is in heaven" when so many of our world long for more than the stuff of earth that plagues them? Maybe the church needs to long for "on earth as it is in heaven" to come alive among all the pain and tragedy and difficulty and betrayal and deceit and oppression so that people might believe that there is more to this life than the "on earth" that they see. Maybe the church needs to think "beyond MY church" long enough to see how selfish we have been pretending that what Jesus might hope for and pray for most for His church is all the self-absorbed stuff going on at "church campuses" every weekend. Maybe the church needs to awaken to the fact that "on earth as it is in heaven" doesn't just pertain to quality programming that meets my family's needs. It is about healing and hope and strength to endure and honesty and truth and freedom being shown to a spouse or a neighbor or a co-worker or a classmate or a homeless man or an orphan because the church lives "on earth as it is in heaven" beyond their own campus in relationship among the people of our world.

The "harvest," after all, is not growing on the campuses where our churches gather. The "harvest," as Jesus described in Matthew 9:37–38, is growing out among the secretive struggles of hurting families and the private sins of passive men and the segregation of hateful grudges and the captivity of ravaging addictions and the oppression of sex trafficking and the exploitation of greedy American bosses in our downtowns as well as among ruthless international thug employers around the world. It's growing out among the many things that are trying to choke it out. The harvest is growing out in the darkness of our world, and crops don't grow without light.

If you take nothing else away from this book, I pray that you will take away a very serious burden and a strong sense of urgency to pray about and process that question of what "on earth as it is in heaven" would look like if you saw it in the city where you live. And don't just pray and process it by yourself either. Why not pray about and process it with leaders of the local church expression of which you are a part? Why not pray about and process that question with five to ten other leaders among the expressions of the church in the city where you live?

And if you decide to pray about and process that question, in order to answer it, you will then have to pray about and process at least one other question:

When Jesus prayed for "on earth as it is in heaven," what was He envisioning and hoping for here?

Be careful before you answer that question quickly. I found in my own life that when I began to pray through and process that question, I began to arrive at answers that were based more in my background and preferences than in the actual teachings of Jesus. I call those my "default." You have a "default" too.

{wanting to be GOOD instead of being willing to GO}

I sat at lunch with a friend not too long ago. He is an accomplished man. He knows many people whom you wish you knew. He has done well for himself and his family. But he told me that he wished our local church family would make the Sunday morning experience more entertaining so that more people would want to come.

I asked him a question. "Who are you discipling right now?" He thought for a moment. He said that he knew that should be more of a priority of his since he was a "Christian," but that he really wasn't ready to do it. He needed to be a little better himself and needed his family to be a little better before he could even think of doing that.

This is a sentiment of many so-called "Christians," I am afraid. Worrying about our own image instead of living in the image of God. Wanting to be good instead of being willing to go. It's like the "default" has become Christianity = self-improvement, rather than Christianity = "As the Father has sent Me, so I am sending you" (John 20:21 NLT). I am afraid that American Christianity has become synonymous with conforming to a certain moral code club that meets on Sunday mornings, rather than following a certain Messiah and living out His ways in and among our culture.

This is evil. And I don't mean to be harsh here, but think about what the word "evil" means. In the Scriptures, I notice what we call "evil" happening when people live in a way opposite to what God intended. And when His church lives in a way opposite to what He intended, it is evil.

Furthermore, if we wait to make disciples, which in my opinion is a mandate for every follower of Jesus, until we are "good enough" to go and make disciples, then when would any of us go? Doesn't this way of thinking ignore the message of the Cross – that His goodness is enough for my badness to be transformed into goodness for the good of others and for the glory of God? And what is the readiness line? When are we "good enough"? This way of thinking is not only incorrect biblically; it is disobedient.

I am in no way saying that our goodness does not matter. I am simply saying that it does not matter if our motivation for goodness is limited to our own personal sense of spiritual fulfillment or to some misguided obligation to God, thinking He won't use me until I am good enough. There are plenty of stories in the Bible that show otherwise. The point is that our goodness is to show His goodness, not to make us feel good about ourselves or to show others how good we are.

Listen to the words of Peter:

But you are not like that, for you are a chosen people. You are royal priests, a holy nation, God's very own possession. As a result, you can show others the goodness of God, for he called you out of the darkness into his wonderful light. Once you had no identity as a people; now you are God's people. Once you received no mercy; now you have received God's mercy. Dear friends, I warn you as "temporary residents and foreigners" to keep away from worldly desires that wage war against your very souls. Be careful to live properly among your unbelieving neighbors. Then even if they accuse you of doing wrong, they will see your honorable behavior, and they will give honor to God when he judges the world.
1 Peter 2:9–12 NLT

We must not stay put in our church buildings wanting to better ourselves. We must go and be the church in our cities allowing God to keep shaping us from the inside out to show His goodness to the world.

I want to challenge the church leader or pastor or whatever you call the clergy (whom we highlight as more important than others in the church, which is not biblical either). Are you equipping people to go and make disciples in their daily lives and around the world, or are you just equipping people to show up and hear you teach or to conform to a moral code that you or some leadership team decided mattered? The former is what was intended. The latter is evil too.

What if God wants to use each and every one of His followers as "farmers" so to speak, cultivating His gospel and love and hope into the hard ground of lives that are immersed in heavy darkness longing for a ray of light and a drop of living water? What if He wants to use His church to do more than add members? What if wants to use His church to bring heaven to earth? Didn't He pray for it—"on earth as it is in heaven"?

{what "on earth as it is in heaven" *doesn't* look like}

Maybe taking a few minutes here to think about what "on earth as it is in heaven" *doesn't* look like would be helpful.

God brought the Jews up out of Egypt and established them in the land we today call Israel. It truly is a land flowing with milk and honey, in the sense that almost miraculously without an ample water supply it grows and exports much of the produce used in Europe, western Asia, and northern Africa. No wonder it is such a sought-after land.

Stick with me on this thought train.

And no wonder God decided to relate closely with this people, despite their waywardness and unfaithfulness (Hosea 1 and 2). No wonder He chose to reveal His presence to and through them, so that the world at that time would see Him, even in some small way. After all, the whole world traveled through that land in some way, since Israel was and still is a land bridge for commerce and trade connecting three continents. No wonder God wanted to show His glory through that people in that land (even ultimately by coming in skin to walk among them and die for the sins of the whole world).

I could go on, but here's the point. God told Israel through the prophet Isaiah that He intended more for them than just to make them "good." He wanted to show His goodness through them as they came and went from that land and to others who came and went through that land.

This is what the Lord says: "Be just and fair to all. Do what is right and good, for I am coming soon to rescue you and to display my righteousness among you. Blessed are all those who are careful to do this. Blessed are those who honor my Sabbath days of rest and keep themselves from doing wrong. Don't let foreigners who commit themselves to the Lord say, 'The Lord will never let me be part of his people.' And don't let the eunuchs say, 'I'm a dried-up tree with no children and no future.'" For this is what the Lord says: "I will bless those eunuchs who keep my Sabbath days holy and who choose to do what pleases me and commit their lives to me. I will give them—within the walls of my house—a memorial and a name far greater than sons and daughters could give. For the name I give them is an everlasting one. It will never disappear! I will also bless the foreigners who commit themselves to the Lord, who serve him and love his name, who worship him and do not desecrate the Sabbath day of rest, and who hold fast to my covenant. I will bring them to my holy mountain of Jerusalem and will fill them with joy in my house of prayer. I will accept their burnt offerings and sacrifices, because my Temple will be called a house of prayer for all nations." For the Sovereign Lord, who brings back the outcasts of Israel, says: "I will bring others, too, besides my people Israel."
Isaiah 56:1–8 NLT

God wanted to blossom "on earth as it is in heaven" among the people of Israel. But according to Paul in Romans 10, they missed it. Why did they miss it? Because they focused on wanting to be good rather than being willing to go. Check it out:

Dear brothers and sisters, the longing of my heart and my prayer to God is for the people of Israel to be saved. I know what enthusiasm they have for God, but it is misdirected zeal. For they don't understand God's way of making people right with himself. Refusing to accept God's way, they cling to their own way of getting right with God by trying to keep the law. For Christ has already accomplished the purpose for which the law was given. As a result, all who believe in him are made right with God.

For Moses writes that the law's way of making a person right with God requires obedience to all of its commands. But faith's way of getting right with God says, "Don't say in your heart, 'Who will go up to heaven?' (to bring Christ down to earth). And don't say, 'Who will go down to the place of the dead?' (to bring Christ back to life again)." In fact, it says, "The message is very close at hand; it is on your lips and in your heart." And that message is the very message about faith that we preach: If you confess with your mouth that Jesus is Lord and believe in your heart that God raised him from the dead, you will be saved. For it is by believing in your heart that you are made right with God, and it is by confessing with your mouth that you are saved. As the Scriptures tell us, "Anyone who trusts in him will never be disgraced." Jew and Gentile are the same in this respect. They have the same Lord, who gives generously to all who call on him. For "Everyone who calls on the name of the Lord will be saved."

But how can they call on him to save them unless they believe in him? And how can they believe in him if they have never heard about him? And how can they hear about him unless someone tells them? And how will anyone go and tell them without being sent? That is why the Scriptures say, "How beautiful are the feet of messengers who bring good news!"
Romans 10:1–15 NLT

If you have read the Book of Acts in the New Testament, then you have read about how the early church, mostly made up of Jews, was unsure about including the Gentiles in on this new glorious Jesus stuff. They clearly had missed what God had been saying all along, in much more than just the words of Isaiah that were included in this chapter. Paul in Romans 10 is presenting the argument that the Jews missed it because of their inward focus on self-righteousness and because of their introspection with regard to personal capability to keep the law. They were so busy trying to be good and live up to this good standing that they perceived themselves having with God, that they missed the "going" and the need to use those "beautiful feet" to take the message of their good God to the world.

Is it just me, or does that sound eerily like the American church?

Don't get me wrong. We send money and people to other nations to tell them the gospel. But what about using our beautiful feet right here in our homes, our neighborhoods, our places of work, and our cities? And what about being careful not to be arrogant even in our going around the world thinking that they need our good American version of Christianity there when God may have in mind to blossom "on earth as it is in heaven" among them in a way unique to their culture.

What if "on earth as it is in heaven" is *not* our keeping the law perfectly, but rather living out His perfect love? What if it is *not* trying to live with a good image pretending that we have it all together, but rather it is living in and among a people, like God did when He became Emmanuel, so that they see the image of the One who made them in His image?

Listen. Are you more concerned about the preservation of an entity or the maintenance of a building or the safety of your kids or the endurance of a tradition or even your own goodness than you are about the mission of God? If so, then you are NOT concerned about "on earth as it is in heaven" blossoming in the city where you live.

{are we willing to do whatever it would take?}

Do you want to be concerned about "on earth as it is in heaven" blossoming in the city where you live? What do you think the local expressions of His church in the city where you live would need to "sow" in order to reap "on earth as it is in heaven" there?

May I suggest three very essential points to consider for this cultivation activity in which we must involve ourselves as farmers of the gospel in our city. And they aren't easy. But they must be considered if we are willing to do whatever it would take to see "on earth as it is in heaven" in our city.

1) Our default instructions for planting might be wrong.

If I went to Lowe's to buy some plants and I didn't know much about what to do with those plants, then I would surely need to read the instructions that come with them with regard to planting and ongoing health. I would not just do it myself with no regard to what might help that plant be healthy (although they do have a money-back guarantee for one year on all of their plants).

Let's say I did decide to read the instructions. And I did exactly what they said. It is well-meaning, of course to do so. But what if someone snuck into Lowe's overnight and replaced all the correct instructions with bad instructions? What if this evil plant-instruction-switcher offered instructions that seemed reasonable and good enough but in the end were not what it took for that plant to be healthy. So, the plant died after a little while.

I fear that this is exactly what has happened in too many of our local church expressions and in too many of our cities. The evil one got us convinced that cultivation really is nothing more than showing up on a campus on Sunday mornings (and even on Wednesday nights if we are really good) and being faithful to give some money to support the budget of this entity of which we are a member. Most people are not malicious. We have simply been fooled, tricked into believing that this is the way of the Master Cultivator. We are victims to a certain extent, but shame on us if we don't awaken to the fact that when we look beyond our church buildings and programs, our cities are not showing signs of becoming anything more than earthly. Signs of heaven are not there. Shame on us if we don't then go to the Master Cultivator and seek further instructions.

Have we just taken what has "always been done that way" and assumed it is what God wanted done?

Our instructions for cultivation may be wrong. God's intent, as you have read so far, was not for His church to just congregate and preserve but rather to go and restore. God's intent was also not, as you have read so far, for us to do this as individual church expressions, but rather to do it together in our cities.

We may need to ask ourselves, if we are not seeing the signs of "on earth as it is in heaven" in our cities, if we listened to the wrong instructions.

2) God's Instructions for cultivation are simple.

In the teachings of Jesus, we see them summarized to simply love God, love people, make disciples as we go daily and as we go into the world. We are to plant the seed of His Word and His love into the hearts of others while continually watering those seeds planted with His love through us within our ongoing relationships. My friend Billy summarizes this through his equipping emphasis www.ApostleFarm.com by simply offering the instructions, "Plant. Water. Repeat." There is wisdom in this.

Paul declared:

I planted, Apollos watered, but God was causing the growth. So then neither the one who plants nor the one who waters is anything, but God who causes the growth.
1 Corinthians 3:6–7 NASB

We plant His love as He loves through us. We plant His hope as we offer our hope to others. We plant His truth as we live out the ways of the One who called Himself "Truth." Every day of our lives as followers of Jesus, may we plant the gospel (the news that God has come near even into our darkness), may we water it with His love through us, and may we repeat this within our various relationships day after day after day. And ultimately, may we do it together as many local expressions of His church being the church together in our city.

3) God's Instructions for cultivation are not easy.

Why? Because following His instructions requires patience, of which we tend to have very little. Patience is like fertilizer. It really stinks to use it, but it has an amazing impact on the outcome when we do.

Could it be that our lack of patience in what God desires for His church with regard to His cultivation process is what makes His instructions for cultivation not that easy? I think so.

You see, it is easy to just add more members to your church. We can come up with strategies for that and make it happen. You can make an event attractive enough that at least for a short time people will come.

What's hard is getting those people who come to make disciples of Jesus with their family members and friends. What's hard is planting the gospel and watering it with love and then having to wait to see any sign of growth.

You don't plant a seed in the ground and then stand by it for an hour expecting to see a plant, do you? Then neither should we impatiently expect to see explosive growth and additional members if we are doing the hard work of cultivation known as making disciples. The growth will come. And when it does, at least typically in agriculture as well as in the stories of Acts, it comes like a harvest—all at once.

We need more focus on followers of Jesus discipling and less focus on local churches adding members. The addition will come in the form of multiplication eventually if we are faithful to cultivate (I am not saying anything here that you don't already intuitively know). The problem is that we are not cultivating, for the most part. You might ask, "How can you say that, Jason?" Consider this.

{who are you discipling?}

I will ask you what I asked my friend over lunch. Who are you discipling? Tell me the story of how you are learning and living the ways of Jesus with a few who are lost as well as with a few who are following Jesus already. Tell me the stories of cultivation of the gospel in your cities. Don't brag on how big your local expression of the church is. Brag on how active they are to cultivate.

If you aren't discipling someone, then you aren't cultivating the gospel in the city where you live. Thus, you are not being the church as Jesus intended. And, you are not serious about unity among followers of Jesus—what Jesus prayed for in John 17—because you are not serious about the purpose that unifies His church—planting the gospel and watering it with love as you walk in ongoing relationships with one another.

If your idea of "church" is anything besides "making disciples who make disciples who make disciples," then I would suggest that you are not serious about cultivating in the city where you live. Ask yourself—am I more concerned about adding members to MY church than I am about seeing "on earth as it is in heaven" throughout our city?

{the bottom line}

Jesus came to show us "on earth as it is in heaven." In His teachings, He made it very clear that love is ultimate, endurance is necessary, and relationship is central. If we want to see "on earth as it is in heaven," then we must right now decide that cultivating beyond MY church (putting the interests of others above our own) is a priority, that patiently cultivating for this unity is necessary, and that relating with one another as followers of Jesus and then together relating with the people of our city is central to our living out the mission of God in our city.

May we not be selfish. May we relate with one another. May we love and not isolate. And may we look to God to grow His church and His kingdom in our city as it is in His city, "on earth as it is in heaven."

In the next few chapters, I want to offer suggestions as to what "on earth as it is in heaven" might look like if it blossomed in the various spheres of our everyday lives.

CONSIDER and CONVERSE:

1. According to what Jason shared in this chapter and in the book so far, what does "on earth as it is in heaven" mean anyway? What might it look like in the city where we live?

2. What is the difference between wanting to be good and being willing to go? Which one best describes us and our local church expression? Why?

3. Are we willing to do whatever it would take to cultivate for "on earth as it is in heaven" in our city? What might it take?

4. How might we have gotten wrong what Jesus intended for His church with regard to purpose and mission?

5. Why does cultivating the gospel and watering it with love that God intended require so much patience?

6. PRAY. Jesus, please help us to be willing to do whatever it takes to sow for "on earth as it is in heaven" in our city. And please expose what we hold dear and what we think we need to do if it does not match up with what You intended for Your church.

chapter 5

thinking and living beyond MY church with my family

I have five kids. These gifts given to us bring so much noise…I mean joy, into our home. Why we were able to even biologically have one child is beyond me. I will never understand why some men and women who so desire to be parents are not given that chance biologically. We were, by God's grace, and we are grateful. And we try to relish all of them in the now of the everyday, in spite of the obvious frustrations that come and in the midst of the crazy declarations uttered across their beautiful red lips.

There is a Bible verse that says something about how blessed a man is whose quiver is full. The Scripture here is referring to kids in the home of their parents like *arrows* in an archer's bag. Someone posing as a Hebrew scholar, important in this story because the Scripture we are referring to is in the Old Testament and the Old Testament was written in its original form largely in Hebrew, told me that a "quiver" refers to five. My training for taking the SAT before college and a little bit of seventh-grade Latin confirm this, and thus even in child-bearing my wife and I are trying to be biblical and blessed.

My wife and I are sobered by the fact that God gave us five kids to disciple—to learn and live His ways with. We do not take lightly the stewardship of their lives. How we pour into these children given to us is central to the intention of God even giving them to us. Moses made this point very well in Deuteronomy 6:

Attention, Israel! God, our God! God the one and only! Love God, your God, with your whole heart: love him with all that's in you, love him with all you've got! Write these commandments that I've given you today on your hearts. Get them inside of you and then get them inside your children. Talk about them wherever you are, sitting at home or walking in the street; talk about them from the time you get up in the morning to when you fall into bed at night. Tie them on your hands and foreheads as a reminder; inscribe them on the doorposts of your homes and on your city gates.
Deuteronomy 6:4–9 The Message

And so while we don't bat anywhere near 1,000 at this, we are trying morning after morning and drive after drive and meal after meal and bedtime after bedtime to position our "arrows" in the bow that is discipling, in order to release them daily to become disciples of Jesus so that we can release them ultimately when they leave our home to fly into life to be disciple-makers of others and eventually their own families. If we learn and live His ways with them now, while coaching them to be learning and living His ways with others even at a young age, then the likelihood of them being the church as Jesus intended and making disciples and being cultivators of the gospel so that new expressions of the church can blossom will be so much greater than if we just "take them to church" on Sundays.

What excites me about those two previous run-on sentences is this— that hopefully our kids will not grow up understanding "church" as a place or an event that they go to but rather a people who follow Jesus and give themselves away together. Will your kids see you just "going to church" or "being the church"? The answer to this question may determine the future of the church in our cities and in our world.

What also excites me about taking seriously how we are discipling our kids is that, hopefully, they won't grow up thinking in terms of MY church but rather in terms of HIS church together in our city. In this I rejoice, because it gives great hope that they and the people they learn and live the ways of Jesus with will one day be leading His church into loving relationships, new expressions, and compassionate service, all the while speaking and demonstrating the gospel so that the world will know the One who was sent.

May I offer five suggestions for how you can think and live beyond MY church with your family? Please note, these are applicable whether you are husband or wife, father or mother, child or sibling, single or married, grandparent or grandchild.

{be a friend rather than expecting friends}

Caleb is not only my son. He is my friend and accountability partner. He is now a young man, and my heart sometimes wells up when I see the man he is becoming trying to break through the little boy body that is now fading behind cut muscles and coordinated movement. He is our detailed, analytical, creative, humorous oldest child, born nine days shy of 9/11 and full of a resolve similar to what it took for New York City to make it through that dark season surrounding his birth.

Call me crazy, but the last words that I whispered in Caleb's ears when we dropped him off for his first day of kindergarten were, "Don't wait for people to be your friend, bud. You be a friend to them first." He smiled with that smile I had seen many times that said without saying he understood what I was saying.

I picked him up from class that day. He was excited to tell me about his day, in particular (like most boys) recess. When I asked him who he had met that day, he was able to mention a few names. I asked him if he had been a friend to someone. (We still ask that on a regular basis.) He replied in a way that did not communicate pride in doing good but rather an excitement at what he saw as a result of goodness. He said there was a little boy that people were not playing with. Caleb went to him and asked if it would be OK to join him and play. The little boy smiled, which he had not been doing. And Caleb smiled as a result.

I have been told that people who are introverts can't do this. They can't be outgoing and be a friend to someone who has not first extended friendship. I would suggest that this is a misunderstanding of what it means to be introverted. Three reasons why:

First, and I have asked several very well-credentialed counselors about this, being introverted does not mean you are not outgoing. If you are wired as an introvert, it has nothing to do with whether you are outgoing. It has everything to do with how you recharge so you can keep going.

Caleb is an introvert. He recharges by playing or reading or thinking or doing whatever he needs to do at that moment alone. If he does not get some alone time, he does not function at optimum level. In that alone time, certainly he is not set to go and be a friend to someone. But that's why God commanded things like Sabbath and rest, so that regardless of how you or I are wired, we can keep going.

Second, being introverted doesn't excuse you from thinking of others first. I am amazed at how we excuse some people from being kind because we say that's just who they are as an introvert. God did not make you grumpy and rude. You can still be a friend.

Third, being introverted doesn't entitle you to treat others like they have interrupted your time. It's one thing to need alone time to recharge. It's another thing to excuse the importance of togetherness because you don't feel like being around someone or to treat someone like they are a bother or are intruding because everyone has a need for friendship.

Because Caleb is an introvert, as much as we keep challenging him to be a friend, while challenging ourselves to do the same, we also witness the times when Caleb treats someone like they have intruded into his space. If I am going to help him think and live beyond himself and beyond a MY church mentality, I need to disciple him in the ways of Jesus with regard to putting the interests of others above self—even when he doesn't feel like it.

Jesus did. Regardless of his temperament. He looked to be a friend. He loved us first. He didn't see our sin as too much of an interruption to take off His royal robe, stand up from His throne, slip into human skin, and then let Himself be nailed along with all our sin to a tree. "Greater love has no one than this that one lay down his life for his friends" (John 15:13 NASB).

{be considerate rather than expecting consideration}

Katey is such sunshine around our house and to so many others. She has this smile that, when she does, you wish, if even for a moment, it was your smile. And she has this laugh that is like a New Orleans snowball on a 99-degree summer day—it just makes you happy all over. Grace is her middle name, but *optimism* may as well be. And so should *compassion*. She already tells us at such an early age that she wants to be a nurse. I am sure we will smile at her as she smiles doing whatever it is that she ends up doing. Happily.

Something else that makes us happy about Katey or KG as I call her (Katey Grace) is how considerate she is. It's like God put this inside her and it comes out regularly, because she has been doing this since she was very little. (She even came out at birth and turned and apologized to Jen for all of the birth pains she caused.)

Seriously, though, when we are changing a diaper, if the baby is fussing, KG leans down into his face and talks goo-goo or displays that infectious smiley, silly face. When someone gets hurt in a basketball game in which she is playing, she is the first on the scene extending a hand and asking if the player is OK. When she wakes in the morning, she opens my eyeglasses and hands them to me in a way that makes them easy to slip onto my face and remedy my can-hardly-see eyes. All of this without being asked. All of this just because she is considerate.

Being kind and considerate is underrated in our culture. Friends and teachers and parents and senators and Starbucks baristas and even that I-don't-want-to-work-here-at-all convenience store clerk can never be too considerate and kind if you ask me. In a world where I along with many others spend our time buried in a smart phone or an iPad, our being considerate extends about as far as our focus does and occurs nowhere near as often as AT&T drops my phone calls.

This is true unfortunately even in church culture, and I have to tell

chapter five

you that I firmly believe that this is due to the way we emphasize kindness and being considerate in our families.

I am not saying that perfect parenting makes perfect kids. And I am certainly not saying that my kids are perfect and don't you wish yours were like mine. I am simply saying that if we don't make being considerate to one another a priority in our families, then we don't need to expect our family members to be considerate in the other arenas of life, including as the church.

Think about how easy it is to pick a side in a fight about an important issue among the people of your local church expression only to find yourselves divided. Now think how often those situations could have been avoided if someone was considerate enough to overcommunicate or move just a bit slower or think first that maybe some need of a person or group of people was causing this issue in the first place and maybe we could meet that need.

Part of growing in oneness with others (like Jesus prayed that we would in John 17) is growing to be more and more considerate of one another. Look for ways to help someone. Don't get so consumed in what you are doing (like I just was while typing) that you don't notice the need of someone else or even notice someone else noticing a need of yours and meeting it (like the flight attendant who just brought me another ginger ale without me asking for it). I will make sure to be considerate and tell her thanks.

I would suggest that some of our being inconsiderate also stems from how inconsiderate we are with ourselves. We expect perfection from our performance when our daily formations are so imperfect. And then we have the same level of expectation for others. We are not considerate with ourselves, so no wonder we are so inconsiderate with one another. We do not let ourselves have room to grow. We do not give ourselves the safety net of grace even though our Gracious Catcher-When-We-Fall does. No wonder we don't allow for others, including our children, the safety to fail and get back up again and grow like we all must do.

As strange as it sounds and as compassionate and considerate as KG can be, there are times, with her sister Abby in particular, that she can offer nothing that even resembles grace. She displays instead an expectation that Abby has asked too much of her or has bothered her one too many times. In those moments, we try to remind her of how significant compassion and grace and relationship are. And she usually relents and repents and is considerate once more.

May we be considerate of others, looking for ways to help without them asking and allowing them the opportunity to grow when they ask too much of us. And may we sow the importance of being considerate within our families so that we may reap children who are considerate as the church.

{be the initiator rather than expecting initiative}

Abby is our princess. Her flowing blonde hair and pale, fair skin and ruby red lips make her doll-like on the outside. And her no-nonsense declarations along with her tender charm and even more tender heart make her princess-like on the inside. I am a new character in her world almost every day. My favorite character is the one she calls Prince Charming. And of course I tell her that there will never be another Prince Charming as charming as me so she doesn't need to worry about dating or trying to find one until she is late into her 20s.

Seriously, though, Abby seems to me to be an initiator. Whether it is her assertiveness to try to get me to play Barbies with her, or her leading some particular form of fun among the neighboring kids in our back alleyway, or "this-is-what-we-are-doing" announcements where she confidently declares the role play of the day for our entire family expecting us to call her by her character name and to associate ourselves with our given character name—whether we like it or not. She makes her wishes known.

Some of this is true about Abby because she is so no-nonsense. But some of it is true because she looks at the moment and decides her next step. While a lot of how Abby is currently an initiator revolves around her personal wishes and preferences, we are hopeful that this characteristic will one day shift beyond just herself and her desires.

I would suggest that encouraging your family members to take initiative is one way that you can help them think and live beyond self and beyond MY church.

And don't do what I tend to do too often and need to quit doing because it is so falsely considerate. Maybe you have done it before too. When you know someone is walking through a hard time which means that they most certainly have needs, but instead of being considerate and looking for an immediate way to meet a need, you say that hollow, I-really-don't-mean-to-act-on-this-in-any-way statement, "Let me know if you need anything."

Don't get me wrong. Every now and then you see friendships where people truly do rely on each other because they trust that when one person asks for help, the other does not think they are asking too much. But it takes time to get to that level of trust and reliance on each other. In fact, it takes more than time. It takes you and me looking to be initiators who actively look to meet someone else's needs, rather than pretending that they will stop and call us in the middle of a crisis.

The same is true with regard to how we should relate with other local church expressions in our cities. If we are truly putting the interests of other local church expressions above our own, then surely we are looking for ways that we can serve one another. We will be burdened when we see another local church expression suffering or struggling or having need, and we will make the effort to help meet that need or help prop them up during times of difficulty. And we should be doing all of this without expecting any pat on the back or any notice of the score or any favor in return.

Are we sowing for this kind of thinking and living in our own life and in the lives of our family members? If not, then why would we expect to see this kind of thinking and living in the life of a local church expression of which our family members are a part?

May we be actively looking for ways to help others, without waiting for them to request the help.

God did this. Paul says in Ephesians 1 that it was His plan before the foundation of the world to go to the Cross. In other words, before He made us and before we chose self over Him and especially before we said we were sorry for betraying Him, He took the initiative to put the strategy in place to restore our broken relationship and then acted on that plan.

That's taking initiative. And if we desire to sow the ways of the King in our kids in hopes that His kingdom ways will be reaped in their daily life, then we better make being an initiator a part of what we are sowing.

{be a listener rather than expecting to be heard}

Ella has the sharpest sense of humor and the strongest playful heart of any two-year-old I have ever been around. Her big eyes and even bigger smile capture your heart. It's clear that one of her core values is "let's have fun together," and it becomes even clearer when you try to interrupt the play time to move on to something else.

The Chick-Fil-A playground has been the site of many a moment like this. The kids were enjoying the hope-they-cleaned-the-sick-kid's-vomit-at-least-one-time-this-month two-story jungle gym and slide along with the other 217 kids that somehow miraculously can cram into a 15-by-15 square-foot space (this is Chick-Fil-A so surely it's miraculous). Their fatigued parents rested with one eye open and one eye closed just outside the glass in the feels-like-a-sleep-number-bed booth. Jen and I always give what we call the "two-minute warning." We got the idea from the NFL. Thanks, guys!

So I walked in to communicate that it's time to go because the "two-minute warning" has already been given, and Ella pounces forward, strands of her blonde hair covering one of her big, beautiful eyes, feet spread apart, one hand on her hip and one hand held assertively in the air with two fingers showing. She declares, "Two more minutes!" Her sly smile and charming twinkle in her one eye that I can see with her head tilted at a 37-degree angle are just enough to wrap me around her pinky finger, and I give in and say, "OK. But that's it." At least she was listening the time before (mimicking my commands is a sign of listening, right?).

My wife and I work hard to remind our kids that listening is really important. Especially listening before speaking. They certainly don't get it right all the time. They are not perfect kids, nor do we imagine them to be. But if we don't sow into them to be listeners, then it is less likely to be reaped in their life and they are unlikely to be known as someone who cares enough to listen.

Ella is two. So, in no way do we expect her to be the premier listener of the universe at this point. I am only telling you this as a point of illustration. We are working hard with her right now on only making her wishes known one time. She obviously does not currently believe that asking one time and then listening for the answer is a very effective method. Probably because she is the fourth out of five and has to fight to get heard. Probably also because she really wants to be heard.

There's this one particular song she likes to listen to. It's called "Kickin' It Old School" by the band called Go Fish. She says the title of the song in a very cute way—Kick Old School, Daddy! Kick Old School, Daddy! Kick Old School, Daddy! ...Kick Old School, Daddy! She really likes this song and dances this really cute head-bobbing, arms moving up and down dance to the song. And she obviously feels like asking for it 329 times in a row will help her listen to and dance to this song.

At this moment, I could bring out this amazing story Jesus told about a lady who was so persistent approaching the king about a matter that the king did what she wanted. This is not the kind of story of support that Ella needs for this habit. She does not need to say what she wants or make her requests known over and over again. The point of that story was not to be selfishly redundant in our declarations so that someone will finally do something about it so we will shut up.

That kind of behavior is only OK in church business meetings or complaining sessions, right? Oh, man. Did I just type that?

You have probably seen it though, right? People who want to be heard or maybe have an agenda they think needs to happen, so they join the loud crowd. It is usually a small group, but because of their selfish, redundant declarations, they are easily heard. And they will keep saying it until someone listens and validates them.

I am not saying there doesn't need to be a safe environment for disagreements to be shared and resolved. There does. I am simply saying that thinking and living beyond myself and beyond MY church includes listening first and declaring second and then listening again and listening some more. Conflicts are never resolved by repeating "Kick Old School, Daddy" over and over and over and over again. They are instead resolved when we listen to one another, put the interests of one another above our own interests, and relate with one another with the goal of walking together in the ways of Jesus "on earth as it is in heaven."

If we model this as a family and create an environment where listening first is emphasized, then I bet that we will be surprised at how well this sowing reaps a healthier church environment in the future.

One note—listening is especially important in conflict. If I don't want my kids to go into conflict with their mind already made up (like what tends to happen in most church conflicts), then I don't as a parent need to go into conversations with them with my mind dogmatically resolved in one way before hearing them out. When the authority figures listen, too, it makes for a much better environment of listening, where our kids know they will be heard if they are respectful, and they can know that our family is a safe environment where issues and struggles can be brought up and worked on together.

Isn't that the kind of family environment we want in both our homes and our local church expressions?

{be grateful rather than expecting someone to always do something greater}

I had to include Noah too. Even though he is not five months old as I write this, I had to tell you about his laid-back personality and his handsome smile. And how every time I change a stinky diaper, and every time I sing this cool "Mm-Thump Went the Little Green Frog" song, and every time I lean down to talk to him after I lock him in his car seat, he smiles at me like he is so grateful that I did that and that I couldn't have done it any better.

You know as well as I do that won't always be the case. As we all get older, we seem to become less and less grateful.

I promise I am not making this stuff up, like some preachers tend to do when they stretch an illustration just a wee bit to fit their need in a sermon. Just as I was typing this chapter, my wife texted me the following message: "Our kids will not learn gratefulness if we are not vocal about ours." When she texted me this, I was writing this chapter while at an airport waiting for a plane. I kid you not! She told me later that night after I was home from my trip what had happened.

It had been a long day for mommy and the Dukes five. Bad naps or no naps from the younger two. Sibling infighting from the two older girls. A bit of disgruntlement from the older boy when a few things didn't go the way he hoped. Small incidences, when combined with multiple incidences throughout the day and then multiplied by five kids, can become a bit overwhelming. On the way home from Caleb's basketball practice, they had gone through the drive-thru for some food from that restaurant that has a marketing campaign led by cows. Apple juice was the drink of choice, even though the cows push their lemonade really hard. Jen got home with the kids, got hands washed, seats filled at the table, and drinks placed before thirsty lips. After taking a sip our princess blurts out, of course in the whiniest tone you could imagine, "I wanted lemonade!"

Jen told me she didn't lose it. And she didn't even pull the don't-you-know-there-are-kids-who-have-to-drink-water-out-of-a-sewage-ditch card, like I at times will do in the frustration of the tenth complaint of the day times four (not five since Noah doesn't really complain much yet). (By the way, our friends at www.water.cc would love to hear from you if you want to help those kids drink clean water. But that's another book or blog post or something later.) What Jen did do was calmly talk to them about gratefulness and how important it was to be grateful for their apple juice instead of complaining about not having lemonade. We could, after all, get lemonade next time.

Now if the story stopped there, I would have wasted your reading time sharing it with you. It gets better.

After Jen encouraged them to be grateful, which we have to do constantly (it's not what you teach one time but what you emphasize all the time that makes a difference), she simply uttered a prayer. "Lord, please help me to be more vocal about how grateful I am for You and what You've done, and please help our kids to learn it more too." Well, about an hour later, God answered her prayer in a very you-asked-for-it, here-it-is way.

Jen had been introduced to a book entitled *Bartholomew and the Oobleck*. She had not read it before. But it was on the couch waiting for the six ears of our three oldest kids to be gripped by its riveting story. And Jen told me they were captivated. I will let you read and enjoy the story for yourself if you have not done so before. But I will tell you this. Jen was holding back heavy tears while light weeping broke through as she was finishing the book. God had used Bartholomew Cubbins to answer Jen's prayer and had in the process taught the kids and her and me (as she told me about it that night) three very important lessons.

One, that we like the King in the Oobleck story need to be willing to own up to our mistakes and say we are sorry. Two, that we like the King in the Oobleck story need to be more grateful and not let our ungrateful wishes of things being greater than they already are cause us to create difficulty for ourselves and others. And three, that God is extremely intentional and patient to teach us gratefulness and show us just how great He is.

If I am going to cultivate into my family to think and live beyond self as well as beyond MY church, then I am going to have to sow seeds of gratefulness over and over and over again, as well as be vocal about how grateful I am for God and for my family and this amazing mission of life in which He has invited us and involved us.

{what this might lead to . . .}

You may have more to add than these five I have suggested, but here is where I hope it ultimately leads for both of our families (yours and ours). Ultimately, I hope it leads to each of our kids becoming a disciple maker rather than just expecting to be discipled.

If we are honest, this is epidemic in church culture. People expect to be taught well, but they don't expect to have to teach others what they are learning. Jesus commanded it, though, in Matthew 28:19–20, when He said:

Go therefore and make disciples of all the nations, baptizing them in the name of the Father and the Son and the Holy Spirit, teaching them to observe all that I commanded you; and lo, I am with you always, even to the end of the age.
Matthew 28:19–20 NASB

How amazing it would be if we thought and lived like making disciples was a part of our daily relationship and loving obedience to our Father in heaven. How amazing it would be if we took Moses' commands seriously in Deuteronomy 6. How amazing it would be if this beyond self and beyond MY church approach to the mission of God and the disciple-making mandate began in each of our homes, among each of our families.

What we would find, I am sure, is that our learning and living the ways of Jesus would be most effective and more than enough when we focus beyond ourselves and beyond MY church to help others learn and live His ways too.

Did you notice something? Nothing suggested in this chapter is limited to or driven by anything that happens on the campus where the local church expression of which you are a part gathers. Why? Because Jesus intended for His church to think and live beyond any one local expression or one campus or the (fill in the blank here with a church name)'s programs. He intended for me to think and live beyond MY church, especially with my family. And He intended for my family to know the One who was sent so that the world would know the One who was sent through the everyday life of my family.

I think He intended the same for you. And especially for the neighbors who live directly around you, which is the focus of the next chapter.

CONSIDER and CONVERSE:

1. As a family, what are some ways that we can look to be a friend rather than waiting for people to be our friend?

2. As a family, how might we be more considerate of one another? How might we be more considerate in our other relationships?

3. As a family, what are some of the relationships in which we need to take the initiative and love and serve without being asked? What might we do when we take this initiative?

4. As a family, do we spend more time talking *at* each other or listening *to* each other? What are some of the relationships in which we know we need to listen more?

5. As a family member, am I known as a grateful person or as a person with selfish expectations who tends to give sharp criticism, whether vocally or just in my own head and heart?

6. PRAY. Jesus, we need You to blossom Your love in us. Only You can shape us to love like You love. We can't do it without You in us and You through us. Please teach us and change us to love like You, making us more aware every day of the times when Your Spirit is prompting us to give ourselves away. And then help us to act on that prompting.

chapter 6

thinking and living beyond MY church with my neighbors

Do you know your neighbor's name? Do they know yours? Do they consider you a friend? I am not talking about just being that neighbor-that-always-invites-me-to-church friend. I am talking about when they are in a crisis, they think about calling on you for help. That kind of friend.

Is all they know of you that you are the neighbor who clicks down your garage door and heads to church stuff? Or is all they know of you that you are the neighbor who is too busy to grill out with them because you are running the grill at the fifth church event this month? Or is all they know of you that you are the neighbor who puts a cause or political sign in your front yard, but you never took the time to engage in conversation with them about the causes on their heart? If so, then they only know you as the neighbor who "goes to church" and "comes from church." They don't know you as the neighbor who is being the church, more specifically who is being their friend.

Listen, I am not holding myself or my family up as the poster child for this. We are trying to grow in wisdom and in action with regard to how we love our neighbors on our street. We are also trying to grow in wisdom and in action with regard to how we love the people that we encounter daily in the rhythms of our everyday life (the way that Jesus intended according to the story called "The Good Samaritan"). Our awareness of others, our "neighbors" so to speak, that we run into along the way every day is crucial as we are loving God and loving people as His church.

But for the sake of our focus in this chapter, let's stick to the folks who live on the street or in the apartment complex or wherever it is that you live. Go ahead right now and ask the Lord to bring specific neighbors to mind. Not so that you can think about how good or bad they are or how much or how little they need to change. Rather, so that you can think about how God needs to change you and grow you to love them like He loves them. While you are praying and pondering on that, let me share two really important lessons that my wife and I have been learning over the last few years that hopefully will encourage you as you are loving your neighbor.

{does the church exist on the street where you live?}

If you only think of the church in terms of place or event or campus, then not only are you thinking of the church in a way that is not mentioned in the New Testament, but you are also thinking of the church in a way that rings hollow to your neighbor.

Think about it. Wouldn't you agree that it is totally inauthentic and totally insincere and totally hollow for me (and you) to go to church events and church programs geared to feed my soul if all the while I am walking by or driving by someone, but I am too busy doing church stuff to be the church to them and possibly even offer them a taste that might feed their soul? Especially if it's the person who lives right beside me or right down the street from me.

I know of many leaders who say God has given them BIG dreams to change the world. And they begin to embark on those endeavors, raising funds and mobilizing groups and even gaining a bit of promotion from news sources that highlight grand charity. But I wonder what their neighbor is thinking. I wonder what my neighbor is thinking. If he or she saw a news report about something "grand" we were doing for other people, would it be authenticated by my already-growing friendship with that person or would it ring hollow because of my neglect of them? They live less than 500 feet from me, and here I am going across town or across the world to share the gospel and offer love.

The hurts and pains and loneliness of my neighbor may not show up on a TV screen the way a bloated stomach of a starving child does, but their hurts and pains and loneliness and the darkness of their life is real too. Those who know me know my heart breaks for that hungry child, especially the orphan and particularly the orphans here in the state of Florida. And my heart needs to continue to break for those orphans and hungry kids, but it also needs to break for my neighbor.

I am not trying to get in your face here, but please hear me out. Please take a look at your calendar. Please examine it to see how often you are "going to church." And then please look at your calendar to see how often you are hanging out with your neighbors. If there is a large disparity between the two, where you are rarely with your neighbor but instead are doing church stuff, then there is a large disparity between you saying you love God and love your neighbor and you doing what you say.

Has it ever crossed your mind that maybe God placed you right there on that street and right there in that home, whatever kind of place it is, for "such a time as this"? That's the lesson we learn from Esther, right? She had beauty and virginity and courage, so God used her right then and there to once again protect the Jews from being eradicated. What if God wants to use you to rescue a neighbor, to encourage a neighbor, to serve a neighbor, or even to be the representative of Jesus that finally moves them into a relationship with Jesus? It could happen.

I would suggest to you that you and I must cultivate for "on earth as it is in heaven" on the streets where we live with the neighbors we live around, or else you and I are not thinking and living beyond self or beyond MY church. And we are especially not putting the interests of our neighbors above our own.

{their house or mine?}

Matthew 9 and 10 have been very meaningful to the shaping of my current view of ministry and disciple making. There, Jesus asserted that He did not come just to help the insiders and cater to the appeasement of the healthy, but rather He came for the outsiders and to offer compassion to the sick. There, Jesus told His followers to pray for workers for the harvest, declaring that they were few in number but that He would send them if we would ask. There, Jesus selected and sent out that first batch of workers for the harvest. The seeds of the kingdom had long been dormant, but they were about to emerge before their very eyes. And He gave them very basic but specific instructions with regard to their living sent. He told them:

Jesus sent his twelve harvest hands out with this charge: "…Go to the lost, confused people right here in the neighborhood. Tell them that the kingdom is here. Bring health to the sick. Raise the dead. Touch the untouchables. Kick out the demons. You have been treated generously, so live generously. Don't think you have to put on a fund-raising campaign before you start. You don't need a lot of equipment. You are the equipment, and all you need to keep that going is three meals a day. Travel light. When you enter a town or village, don't insist on staying in a luxury inn. Get a modest place with some modest people, and be content there until you leave. When you knock on a door, be courteous in your greeting. If they welcome you, be gentle in your conversation. If they don't welcome you, quietly withdraw. Don't make a scene. Shrug your shoulders and be on your way. You can be sure that on Judgment Day they'll be mighty sorry—but it's no concern of yours now."
Matthew 10:5–15 The Message

Many points and conclusions can be drawn from this rich section of Scripture. However, I wanted to point out only two things. Notice what Jesus says in verse 6 again and how Eugene Peterson paraphrases it: "Go to the lost, confused people right here in the neighborhood." Their neighborhood. In other translations, Jesus specifically mentions other people groups besides Israel in verse 5, but then in verse 6 He tells them to not go there before they go here. To not go far before they go near.

It became trendy a few years ago for student groups to quit traveling so far for mission service projects and to instead pick a neighborhood in the city where they lived. I am not sure if that wasn't driven by the economy or if it was just the Spirit of God reminding them that home was important too. Either way, I have talked to students who have told me that it had a big impact on them making them aware of needs right here among their friends and neighbors in their city.

I would take it a step further to challenge us all not to just look around our cities for the needs, which we will focus on in a later chapter, but also to look right on our blocks, right on our streets, right in our apartment complexes, right where we live.

We need to go here so that when we go there the people here do not think poorly of our going there, as well as thinking poorly of our not going here. Because if they do, then they will not trust us as sincere or caring except when it is noticed by the rest of our "church friends."

The second point from that Matthew 10 text that I want to point out was pointed out to me a short time ago. My friend Tres said something very significant. He asked me: "Did you notice that in Matthew 10 Jesus told them to go to their house? If that's the strategy, then why do we spend so much time expecting people to come to ours?"

We had taught that point as a local church family for some time when I heard Tres say that, but I had not heard it put as concisely and pointedly. And it is true, isn't it? In church culture, we build buildings with the *Field of Dreams* mentality (if we build it, they will come). And while that may be true to some extent, true in the sense that people do come, for whatever reason, the fact that people might come if we build something doesn't mean that is what Jesus intended.

Listen. I am not declaring that we don't need to build stuff. That's between you and the Lord for your local expression of the church. I am simply saying that if a new building is our primary "outreach" strategy, then we are not following the mission strategy Jesus described in Matthew 10. I would suggest that we are not as "outreach" oriented as we think. We may be very inward in our thinking, disregarding the very people whom we live beside for the sake of a building to which we think they should drive.

chapter six

What would happen if, as I wrote earlier, we didn't lose their trust by going far and never going near? What would happen if we loved them? Befriended them? And not for the sake of adding numbers to our local church expression, but rather for the sake of them finding their way in Christ and experiencing "on earth as it is in heaven" with us, regardless of what local church expression they ever connect with. What would happen if we earned their trust so much that they didn't mind it if we did ask them to join us for a worship gathering one Sunday morning? But what would happen if, beyond inviting them to "our house," they trusted us enough to invite us into theirs?

Again, I am not the poster child for this, but I will share one simple story with you from our street that may encourage you as you are processing this thought.

Scott and Martha have become friends of ours. We are excited for a new job opportunity for Scott, but we are saddened that it is in Denver, because we felt like we were just beginning to grow in friendship and even experience a bit of "on earth as it is in heaven" with them. They have three wonderful kids, and our kids totally dig the time with them.

When they first moved two houses down from us just about a year and a half ago, our connection started slowly. There were some waves, some byes, some good to meet you agains. But finally, after they had lived there for about six months, Scott and I went beyond just small talk. We discovered that we both appreciated a new friend and we both liked basketball. It just so happened that his favorite team, Syracuse, was playing one of our favorite teams, Florida, in a men's college basketball game in Tampa, so I invited him to go with me.

Our friendship continued to grow. Within a few weeks, Scott's family was heading out of town. Scott called me and asked if my son Caleb would take care of their dogs while they were gone for three days. I promise I am not trying to make too much of this, but what happened next meant a lot to me. Scott asked us to come over to show us all Caleb would need to do, and he gave us the keys to their house and the code to their garage.

Maybe that's not a big deal to you, but I don't take it lightly. Scott giving us the key and the code was an indication that he trusted us. He invited us to his house. It was no longer just us inviting him and his family to our house. We were actual friends.

Does that describe the way you are with your neighbor? I hope so. We are trying to grow more and more in trust with our neighbors. Not so that I can "grow MY church." Sincerely. That's not the motivation. Rather, so that we can know love and give love as we grow in friendship with our neighbors, in hopes that if they don't know Jesus they might or if they do that they'll know Him more, and ultimately so that we can experience "on earth as it is in heaven" right here on our street. No matter what local church family any of them connect with—if they ever do.

Now I am not saying that I don't care if they never connect with a local church expression. I am simply suggesting this—that thinking and living beyond MY church with my neighbors is not about them coming to my house or to the "house" where our local church expression gathers, but rather it is about getting to be the church to them right here on our street and in their house. If you and I don't commit to thinking and living beyond MY church with our neighbors, then we have no hope of seeing "on earth as it is in heaven" on our street and furthermore no hope of seeing it in our city.

{OK. I'll do it, but how?}

So you want to try it? Or maybe you already do it, but do you want to hear a few ideas anyway? Here are a few suggestions as to how we can think and live beyond MY church with our neighbors. These are just some practical ways that we can make new friends and develop friendships as we show Christ's love to our neighbors right on our street:

1) move-in treats

   Pretty simple. Someone moves in, and you bake and take them some cookies. You also give them a card welcoming them to the neighborhood that includes your cell number and email and Facebook name, in case they might ever need help. Assure them that it's OK if they contact you.

2) book clubs

   Folks who are a part of our local church expression have started book clubs with their neighbors that have been amazing catalysts for lasting friendship. Typically the topics have revolved around marriage or parenting or money or encouragement, but they have sometimes studied books of the Bible. We have found that people are not estranged to that notion, and they enjoy the chance to read the Scriptures with others. But do both. It's great to read the books and then converse about them, learn stuff and live it out together.

3) grill out swaps

   Pretty simple again. Decide certain nights every month that you want to grill out together as neighbors. Then take turns whose house you do it at. Each person brings their own supply of whatever is being grilled, a side dish or a dessert, and a beverage. And then eat and converse and laugh and encourage one another together.

4) date nights

If you or your spouse are going out, invite a neighboring couple to join you. For dinner or dessert or an activity or all of it. Regardless, it is a chance to connect over real life. And connecting over real life can become pretty significant in a person's life. Just ask the woman at the well (John 4).

5) movie nights

Surely someone on the street has either a super jumbo-size television or maybe even access to a portable screen and projector. Organize a movie night for the folks that live on your street. Make popcorn. Bring out blankets and chairs. Watch the movie and then have dessert together; converse and connect.

6) contact info

Simple. Write your cell number and email and Facebook name and Twitter name and the name of your carrier pigeon if you have one and deliver it to the neighbors on the street where you live. Tell them you just wanted them to have it in case they ever needed anything and that you are thankful to be their neighbor.

7) cause invitations

Maybe the local church family of which you are a part is focusing on some specific need in the city or around the world. Whatever it is, take a flier or give them a card with the Web site on it and invite them to serve with you, whether literally there in the city or from a distance as you collect money or items to send across the globe. You will be surprised at how many people want to join you in the effort.

8) Christmas play (drama)

Yes, I said Christmas play. A friend of mine, as he was connecting with his neighbors, asked them one fall season if that coming Christmas they wanted to do a neighborhood Christmas play. Almost all of them said yes. They owned different parts of it, each family taking a part of the Christmas story. The only requirement was that they had to tell it from the actual Scriptures from Matthew and Luke. That got all of them in the Scriptures together, and both the play as well as the conversation that followed were beautiful.

9) kids' connections

Do your kids play sports? Drama? Dance? Do your neighbors' kids? See if y'all can do it together, ride together, support them together, be team parents together. It'll be fun!

10) girls' stuff

The women on the street where you live, if they are like a lot of women at least here where we live, don't get much of a breather. Especially if they are moms. So, plan a girls' night out once a month and go as neighbors. Take turns doing stuff that allows for recreation and eating and conversation. And have fun taking a short break with one another.

11) guys' stuff

Same thing as the "girls' stuff," except it's stuff guys like and at least a little bit of belching and trash talk about how the team you cheer for is better than the one they cheer for.

What are some of your ideas? Please share them at www.beyondMYchurch.com. Notice again that none of this happens on a church campus somewhere. They are all actions that go beyond MY church. And they are all actions that cultivate love for one another, which Jesus declared to be a sign of His ways showing up right there in your neighborhood!

One additional note—the reason some "Christians" shy away from some of these types of suggestions is because we have gotten so used to only hanging out with "Christians" that we don't even know how to interact with people who aren't (assuming that some of your neighbors are not following Jesus, which is likely). Well, Jesus wants to make you to become "fishers of men" (Mark 1:17). So, if you don't have any lost friends who would call you their friend, then you need to ask yourself if you are surrendering to be made what He said He would make you to be if you follow Him. And, you need to remember that you probably have plenty of connection points with your neighbors. It's just that if they don't follow Jesus, then "church" may not be one of them. But that's OK. You should have more to talk about than "church stuff." Try just *being the church* for a change. Talk about real life. And don't be afraid to talk about Jesus like He is leading and shaping the daily rhythms of your life instead of just someone whose "house" you visit on Sundays. Try it! You might like it.

CONSIDER and CONVERSE:

1. Do our neighbors see us "going to church" or know us as people who are "being the church"?
2. Which is true—our local church expression equips followers of Jesus to invite people to "our house" or equips followers of Jesus to befriend and love and earn trust so that others invite us into their houses and their lives?

3. What are some specific needs right here on the streets where we live? What are our neighbors' names and what might encourage them the most?

4. Do our neighbors even know how to contact us if they needed something?

5. What are some ideas for how we can connect with and grow in relationship with our neighbors right here on the streets where we live?

chapter 7

thinking and living beyond MY church in our city

One time, a pastor told me this—"MY church would grow if we would add a covered drive-up area where people could pull up and drop people off during bad weather." Does anyone other than pastors think like that? *Seriously*. I just listened, trying to respect his opinion. I have to admit it was *not* easy.

I had never read anywhere in the Bible or outside of the Bible that covered drive-ups were essential to "church growth." I thought that getting people to cross the street away from a church building into their community (regardless of the weather) would be more effective (being the church) than pulling out of the street up under a covered drive-up during inclement conditions to drop people off for just "going to church." Just my opinion, though.

May I suggest that this kind of thinking, while maybe not as specific as the covered drive-up example, is pretty common in church culture? Thinking and living like everything "church" happens at a central place or campus. And that word *place* is the key. We say the church is people, but we live like the church is place. And "church" happens "at MY church" so everyone in the city should come there.

Here's the problem: Jesus called His church to go. He did not intend for us to expect the lost to come. He did not intend for us to centralize. He intended for us to decentralize. This does not mean that we should not gather. We should. But we should gather for the same reason that the "gathering" verse says we gather (you know the one people always quote when they argue about this sending is more important than gathering thing).

Let us hold fast the confession of our hope without wavering, for He who promised is faithful; and let us consider how to stimulate one another to love and good deeds, not forsaking our own assembling together, as is the habit of some, but encouraging one another; and all the more as you see the day drawing near.
Hebrews 10:23–25 NASB

chapter seven

Did you see that? We are not to forsake "our own assembling together." I get that. But did you see why? Because we need to encourage each other with the reminder that the One who gave us our hope is not wavering in the giving or the completing of that hope. And because our coming together (v. 25) gives us the opportunity to leave (v. 24). In other words, it gives us the chance "to stimulate one another to love and good deeds," not only amongst ourselves, but also in the city where we live.

This was so desperately needed for those to whom Hebrews was written (or spoken since it was probably a sermon written down). They were beginning to face persecution for their faith, doing love and good deeds in and among the people of their city. As a result, some of them began to ponder isolation and possibly throwing in the towel on this Jesus stuff, discouraged that it wasn't worth it. They needed to gather so they could leave and keep living sent as a letter of Christ's love right there in the communities where they lived.

So before we quote those verses as support for why our gathering is so much more important than anything, maybe we should ask ourselves two questions. Are we actively loving the people of our city enough that some are welcoming it while others critique and even persecute it? And, do we need to gather because of the support we need from each other to keep loving and giving ourselves away into our city? The answer to the first determines whether we even need to ask the second.

The point is this. If your "church" activity is limited to what goes on at one piece of property in the city where you live, then you are not thinking and living "beyond MY church" in the city where you live.

Am I so focused on MY church that I think more about what happens on the church property than I do about what happens out in the community?

Don't we know good and well that Jesus wants us to do more than turn off the streets into church buildings? Don't we know that He wants us to take His love into the streets and corners of our city? Are we willing to cross the street away from our church buildings, or are we waiting and expecting the people of our city to come to us, to be attracted—for whatever reason—to show up where our local church expressions gather?

{loving the city where you live}

It's all in how you look at it, isn't it? Not just how you think and live as the church, but even in how you view the city where you live.

So when you think about the city where you live, do you think overcrowded and traffic jams? Do you think small and peaceful? Do you think clean and well-kept, or dirty and poor infrastructure? Do you think it's "just where I live" or something like "wish I didn't live here"? Do you think, "You stay on your side of the street, and I will stay on mine"?

Regardless of what you think, you do live there. You do work there. You do shop there. You do recreate there. You do drive there. So, therefore, you have been invited to partake in the mission of God right there smack in the midst of the city where you live.

When Jesus saw the crowds pressing against Him, He didn't think about going to a less crowded neighborhood. Instead, He was moved with compassion (check out Matthew 14:14).

I am amazed at the number of times I hear people claim that if they were just in the right place they would be able to do what God wants them to do. My contention is that if you are not loving God and loving people and making disciples and giving yourself away right where you currently are, what good would a move and a change of venue do? And if you have big dream for missions, claiming that you have a passion for this people or that people, but you don't demonstrate a compassion for the people currently around you, then I would contend that the person you really have a passion for is yourself.

We get so caught up thinking about how we want to serve that we miss the many opportunities daily to serve right where we are. This isn't

chapter seven

so much about the "where." This is about the "who" that live in the "where" wherever the "where" is.

So, as we desire to think and live "beyond MY church" in the city where we live, may we consider the "who," the people, that are included in the following areas (the "wheres") of our city.

{where there is money and where there is not}

In the city where our family lives, there is extreme wealth as well as extreme poverty. That is probably the case where you live too. We have within about a nine square mile area people such as Shaq, Sylvester Stallone, Tiger Woods, and the inventor of the airbag. And we have people living in tents and families scraping by to keep a hotel room and men living in homes where the indoor plumbing is not even functional. We live where there is money and where there is not.

Thus, if we are to be the church in our city as Jesus intended, we need to go and be the church both where there is money and where there is not. You do too. And as you do, you will plant the gospel, water it with your love and presence, and possibly see new expressions of His church blossom among the rich and poor alike.

I have a friend who hangs around with people who have a lot of money. He also has a lot of money. I am not naming him here because he has a lot of money and wouldn't want to be highlighted as having a lot of money. Anyway, he hangs where there is a lot of money. He does not see this as either good or bad. It is just his reality.

What he does see, however, is the opportunity to love and serve and influence people who live for the financial bottom line to see a whole new bottom line. One that focuses beyond themselves. When it comes to being the church, my friend is not leaving out this very important sphere of his daily life—cultivating the gospel among the rich.

Kelly spends some of her days in a community near us where the level of poverty is almost unmatched in all of central Florida. She and her family have sensed the Lord leading them to befriend the people of this community. With more than just a service project and a handout, they are cultivating the gospel there through love and friendship and spending time relating with and learning from the people of this community. She and her family do not think they have a lot to offer. They believe they have a lot to gain from the beautiful people of this community. But it is not personal gain that compels them to go there. It is love and relationship.

Many of the kids there are longing for affection and activity and a meal. So, Kelly takes her kids to hang out with the families in that impoverished community. She and her family have even pondered moving there. We will see what happens there. In the meantime, they are hugging and exercising with and feeding the kids of that community. All the while, growing in friendship with the kids and parents. It is a beautiful thing—living the gospel among the poor.

If we are to think and live "beyond MY church" in our city, then we have to be willing to go where there is money and where there is not. We also need to be careful not to become starry-eyed when we see wealth and the potential ways it could help us if the wealthy would give us some. This is dangerous because of the favoritism it can cause us to show. And favoritism is like an infection for MYchurchitis. You want to avoid that infection and the thinking and living that it causes. As James wrote the early church:

My dear friends, don't let public opinion influence how you live out our glorious, Christ-originated faith. If a man enters your church wearing an expensive suit, and a street person wearing rags comes in right after him, and you say to the man in the suit, "Sit here, sir; this is the best seat in the house!" and either ignore the street person or say, "Better sit here in the back row," haven't you segregated God's children and proved that you are judges who can't be trusted? Listen, dear friends. Isn't it clear by now that God operates quite differently? He chose the world's down-and-out as the kingdom's first citizens, with full rights and privileges.

This kingdom is promised to anyone who loves God.
James 2:1–5 The Message

{where it is safe and where it is not}

In the book *Live Sent*, I spent an entire chapter sharing my suggestions on how following Jesus is not safe. I am amazed at how so many in church culture arrived at the notion that it is safe. It's like we remember the times the people of the Bible got to walk across a sea on dry land with a natural aquarium on each side, but we forget the people who were beheaded.

It is a lie of church culture that the safest place to be is in the center of God's will. It is not safe there. Secure. But not safe. And there's a difference. Secure means held regardless of the ending. Safe brings the expectation that no danger will come. Ask Rack, Shack, and Benny (as Veggie Tales calls the guys who faced King Neb and the fiery furnace) if they felt safe or if they felt secure. Their faith declaration is staggering, standing before the fire that would most certainly consume them.

Shadrach, Meshach, and Abednego answered King Nebuchadnezzar, "Your threat means nothing to us. If you throw us in the fire, the God we serve can rescue us from your roaring furnace and anything else you might cook up, O king. But even if He doesn't, it wouldn't make a bit of difference, O king. We still wouldn't serve your gods or worship the gold statue you set up."
Daniel 3:16–18 The Message

That's not feeling safe. That's resting secure. And we in church culture must surrender the need to be safe in order to think and live "beyond MY church" in our cities. We must surrender the need to personally be safe, and we must surrender the need even for our kids to be safe and happy. The darkness of our cities being overcome with His light depends on it.

Why is it that we treat certain parts of our cities with fear, as though they are our enemies out to get us. This is a lie of Satan! He is winning this battle all too often, making the church scared to do exactly what Jesus said we must do, because Satan has convinced us that it is unsafe to go and love the people of those parts of our cities.

Dietrich Bonhoeffer is quoted in *Life Together: The Classic Exploration of Faith in Community* as saying:

"Jesus Christ lived in the midst of his enemies. At the end all his disciples deserted him. On the Cross he was utterly alone, surrounded by evildoers and mockers. For this cause he had come, to bring peace to the enemies of God. So the Christian, too, belongs not in the seclusion of a cloistered life but in the thick of foes. There is his commission, his work."

In that same work, Bonhoeffer quotes Martin Luther as saying:

"The kingdom is to be in the midst of your enemies. And he who will not suffer this does not want to be of the Kingdom of Christ; he wants to be among friends, to sit among roses and lilies, not with the bad people but the devout people. O you blasphemers and betrayers of Christ! If Christ had done what you are doing who would ever have been spared."

Has the church settled on the belief that safely riding to and residing at the places where we gather is enough? Have we convinced ourselves that when Jesus died on the Cross, that this is what He had in mind for His church?

The issue is this, and I am saying this from a place of deep conviction, not a place of strong performance. The issue is that we as the church are not treasuring what Jesus treasures. He treasures people. We treasure possessions. Whether it is losing an iPhone or losing my "self," we are more afraid of losing our personal treasures than we are willing to give love to the persons who are treasures to God. Jesus said:

Be generous. Give to the poor. Get yourselves a bank that can't go bankrupt, a bank in heaven far from bank robbers, safe from embezzlers, a bank you can bank on. It's obvious, isn't it? The place where your treasure is, is the place you will most want to be, and end up being.
Luke 12:33–34 The Message

If the people of our city, whom God loves, are also treasures to His church, as they are to God, then His church will go and be His church in and among the people of our city, whether it's safe or not. In order to think and live "beyond MY church" in our city, we must trust that we are secure in Him, no matter what, and go to give His treasure of love into the treasures whom He loves.

{where there's a job and where's there's not}

Are you being the church in the marketplace? I am not talking about anything like turning God's house of prayer into a den of robbers. We do that probably more than we think already, pushing our own budgets and agendas more than God's. Nonetheless, I am suggesting cultivating the gospel and watering it with love while you are at work, at school, out to eat, at the grocery, at the local gym—anywhere there is a job.

I would suggest that if you and I are not consciously aware of the opportunities to be the church to others in the midst of the marketplace, then we are not living His mission as Jesus intended, and we are totally missing the chance to be the church a good 40 to 80 hours a week.

Maybe you are a part of a local church expression, and your pastor does not emphasize this kind of living. Or maybe it is emphasized, but the pastor and leadership don't equip you to do it. Here's what you should do.

Begin to pray for wisdom. "Lord, please help me understand how to be the church in the marketplace daily. Please give me ideas. Please open my eyes to listen to my coworkers, to notice the mood of waiters and waitresses, and to look into the eyes of the people I am around in the marketplace. Lord, please give me wisdom on how to cultivate Your gospel and water it with love as I live daily in the various elements of the marketplace in our city."

Then, listen to what He whispers to your heart (however He prompts you) and do what He says.

And then, share the story with other folks living sent in the marketplace, encouraging them to do the same.

Then ask the pastor if you and this crew of folks being the church in the marketplace can in the fall and spring lead groups that equip and inspire people to be the church in the marketplace—where there is a job.

Josh is the general manager of a local cafe. He not only leads his team to make some of the best sandwiches and salads and espressos in all of Metro Orlando, he also leads them to care about every single customer and to care about their local community. They give away all of their net profit back into the community. And they consistently are inviting customers to serve locally and globally with them. Last year, they were a part of a group of organizations that helped to raise $11,000 to put a well in an Ethiopian village, and they raised money and clothes week after week for a local ministry to the homeless. Customers not only gave, they went to serve with that local homeless ministry and several local schools the cafe serves and more. And some of them began to follow Jesus, the One who compels us to live beyond self and beyond MY church. All because a guy who runs a cafe did more than just run a cafe.

Don't forget, though, to be the church to those who wish they had a job.

Joy also serves with that local homeless ministry. She works as a nurse. But she also gives herself away into her city among people who have no jobs. Almost every Tuesday she helps care for homeless men, women, and children who come in for medical care, showers, haircuts, IDs, dental help, clothes, a meal, job placement, and more. She is cultivating the gospel and watering it with love. She is thinking and living beyond MY church in our city.

{where the least become of greatest concern}

I would suggest that in order for the church to think and live "beyond MY church" in our cities, we must not only be willing but even eager to think and live as though the least (the overlooked and ignored and poor and broken) become of greatest concern to us. Taking it one step further, I would suggest that in order for the church to think and live "beyond MY church" in our cities, we must do more than a service project for the least. We need to be their friends, become friends, do life together.

Read what the prophet Isaiah challenged the people with in Isaiah 58:

"Shout! A full-throated shout! Hold nothing back—a trumpet-blast shout! Tell my people what's wrong with their lives, face my family Jacob with their sins! They're busy, busy, busy at worship, and love studying all about me. To all appearances they're a nation of right-living people—law-abiding, God-honoring. They ask me, 'What's the right thing to do?' and love having me on their side.

But they also complain, 'Why do we fast and you don't look our way? Why do we humble ourselves and you don't even notice?' "Well, here's why: "The bottom line on your 'fast days' is profit. You drive your employees much too hard. You fast, but at the same time you bicker and fight. You fast, but you swing a mean fist. The kind of fasting you do won't get your prayers off the ground. Do you think this is the kind of fast day I'm after: a day to show off humility? To put on a pious long face and parade around solemnly in black? Do you call that fasting, a fast day that I, God, would like?

"This is the kind of fast day I'm after: to break the chains of injustice, get rid of exploitation in the workplace, free the oppressed, cancel debts. What I'm interested in seeing you do is: sharing your food with the hungry, inviting the homeless poor into your homes, putting clothes on the shivering ill-clad, being available to your own families. Do this and the lights will turn on, and your lives will turn around at once. Your righteousness will pave your way. The God of glory will secure your passage.

Then when you pray, God will answer. You'll call out for help and I'll say, 'Here I am.' "*If you get rid of unfair practices, quit blaming victims, quit gossiping about other people's sins, if you are generous with the hungry and start giving yourselves to the down-and-out, your lives will begin to glow in the darkness, your shadowed lives will be bathed in sunlight. I will always show you where to go. I'll give you a full life in the emptiest of places—firm muscles, strong bones. You'll be like a well-watered garden, a gurgling spring that never runs dry.*"
Isaiah 58:1-11 The Message

Did you notice it? Many of you reading this do some of what Isaiah spoke about. There was one that I fear trips many of us up, though: *"Inviting the homeless poor into your homes."*

What if we did?

Rather than taking this as a new form of legalism, like you are not even a follower of Jesus if you don't do this, maybe we should do what Isaiah said. He wasn't just giving a new formula for being good. He was asserting that God intended for His people, whether rich or poor, homeless or housed, family or stranger, to know each other. To relate. To be friends.

Maybe that's one of the simplest but most apt ways to describe "on earth as it is in heaven"—RELATING WITH ONE ANOTHER. Loving each other. Being loving, honest, open, loyal friends.

"I'm no longer calling you servants, because servants don't understand what their master is thinking and planning. No, I've named you friends, because I've let you in on everything I've heard from the Father."
John 15:15 *The Message*

Jesus described those who lived out "on earth as it is in heaven" and even lived as though already ready for heaven in this way:

Then the King will say to those on his right, "Enter, you who are blessed by my

chapter seven

Father! Take what's coming to you in this kingdom. It's been ready for you since the world's foundation. And here's why: I was hungry and you fed me, I was thirsty and you gave me a drink, I was homeless and you gave me a room, I was shivering and you gave me clothes, I was sick and you stopped to visit, I was in prison and you came to me."

Then those "sheep" are going to say, "Master, what are you talking about? When did we ever see you hungry and feed you, thirsty and give you a drink? And when did we ever see you sick or in prison and come to you?"

Then the King will say, "I'm telling the solemn truth: Whenever you did one of these things to someone overlooked or ignored, that was me—you did it to me."
Matthew 25:36-40 The Message

Do we remember that we ourselves are also "least" masterpieces because we were loved, not because we are lovable, that God has richly bestowed His love upon us? We must give away what has been given to us as though we can relate to and learn from and grow with the "least" of our cities, remembering that we ourselves continue to be desperate for a near and gracious love.

Besides, our love for the least is not just an indicator of whether we love others well. It is an indicator of whether we love God. Being active in "MY church" activities is not an indicator of spiritual maturity. Loving others and putting the interests of others above my own is. *"But the one who keeps God's word is the person in whom we see God's mature love. This is the only way to be sure we're in God"* (1 John 2:5 *The Message*). Wow! The NASB translates the end of verse 5 in this way—"By this we know that we are in Him." The indicator "to be sure we're in God" is mature love. Living beyond myself and beyond MY church.

What are we scared of risking if we love others around us every day and love the people of our cities like this? What are we afraid of losing? What are we holding more dear, giving our love to? John went on later in 1 John 2 to say this:

Don't love the world's ways. Don't love the world's goods. Love of the world squeezes out love for the Father. Practically everything that goes on in the world—wanting your own way, wanting everything for yourself, wanting to appear important—has nothing to do with the Father. It just isolates you from Him.
1 John 2:15–16 The Message

Isolation from the Father? That doesn't sound like "on earth as it is in heaven." That sounds like hell.

Not to be over the top, but if the local church expression of which you are a part does not think and live "beyond MY church" in the city where you live, then you may look more like hell than like heaven. Is that OK for you?

Author Dorothy Day is quoted as saying: "I really only love God as much as I love the person I love the least."

Ouch!

{crossing the street}

Josh, the general manager of the cafe I mentioned earlier, told me this story:

He had come into the cafe for coffee and an occasional sandwich. Josh would talk to him but he admitted to me later that at times it would be annoying if he would sit for too long. The seating capacity in the cafe wasn't much, and every seat counted toward keeping the doors open during a lunch rush that hadn't been that spectacular during this down economy. Josh also admitted to me later that he regretted ever being annoyed at all.

"He" lived across the street in the woods in a homeless camp where living rooms and bedrooms and grilling spaces are scattered among lean-tos and plastic tarps and makeshift tents. The tall trees served as shaded air conditioning and a bit of privacy from the Highway 50 traffic of more than 120,000 cars a day. Very often ignored, especially by us (we didn't know they were there for the longest time, so tucked back in the woods, their presence was not easily discernible), men and women without a "house" called the woods their home. Were they really "homeless" then? Or just "houseless"?

We know Scott, a local pastor and hero among these beautiful people who lived in the woods. He calls them "structurally challenged" with a compassionate and familiar smile. He has done more for them than anyone. We are learning from him. He crosses the street all the time to love on these folks who are more commonly hated by city officials and ignored by those who call themselves a "church."

And the "he" we are referencing here was ignored by us. Until the local news brought him to the forefront of everyone's mind.

A local teen, possibly seeking drug money, wandered into the "home" (woods) of these homeless one evening. That teen got into an argument with "him," authorities would say later. That teen left only to return with a form of judgment that would not only end the argument but would also end his opponent's life. The man who enjoyed a cup of coffee and a little small talk in the cafe was murdered. Right across the street from the cafe.

He had come to us. We had not gone to him. *Ever.*

We had not crossed the street.

{the bottom line}

So, basically, it seems to me that God is saying to His people who have been very busy planning for drive-under overhangs for inclement weather and strategizing about how to make Sunday morning gatherings bigger and better and spending a lot of time just studying about Him that He intended for more than MY plans and MY strategies and even MY study time. He actually wants us to do what He said, what His Scriptures teach us about His ways.

For example, to do more than just admit that there are homeless poor in our community, but to "invite the homeless poor into our homes." To love the people of our cities where there is money and where there is not, where it is safe and where it is not, where there's a job and where there's not, where the least become of greatest concern. And we have to cross the streets in front of the campuses where our local church expressions gather to do this.

Will you think and live "beyond MY church" in the city where you live? Will you cross the street?

Imagine what would happen if every local church expression in the city where you live made this a priority rather than putting so much effort into growing their own thing. What kind of "on earth as it is in heaven" would we see then? We will focus on that in the next chapter.

CONSIDER and CONVERSE:

1. When you think of "church," do you only think of what happens on the campus of the local expression of the church with which you are connected (entity), or do you think of the church alive in the city (evidence)?

2. When you look around your community, what are some ways that you and the people you do life with closely could begin to "cross the street" and grow in love and friendship with others in our city?

3. What would a "transformed community" look like in our city? What might you have to cultivate there for that to blossom?

chapter 8

thinking and living beyond MY
church together with other
local church expressions

When you think about the church in the city where you live, do you think buildings that dot street corners? Do you think gatherings at rented retail fronts or schools? Do you think competition, all these local churches marketing for the same clientele to keep each of their budgets afloat? Do you think of bottom lines in terms of MY church being successful or in terms of HIS church being alive together in and for this city?

MY-church-being-successful kind of thinking will squelch the Spirit of God from fully blossoming the work of God in the city where you live. HIS church being alive together may usher in the kingdom, "on earth as it is in heaven" as it were. Which one do you want to happen?

Might I suggest that when you and the leadership of the local church expression of which you are a part envision and implement for ministry in the city where you live, if it is focused only on the one church family of which you are a part, then you are not thinking and living beyond MY church in the city where you live.

When you think of "success" with regard to the church in the city where you live, if you only think of "MY church" (just that one local church expression of which you are a part), then you are not thinking of "the church" in the city where you live like Jesus thought about her and prayed for her.

Jesus prayed that His bride would live in love and purity. One of the very significant expressions of "love" at least as is indicated in His prayer in John 17 is most demonstrated in the way that local church expressions unite to be the church together to the city. It's like Jesus might actually want us to take seriously what He prayed (to be of one heart and mind) and to live out what Paul admonished for us:

In light of all this, here's what I want you to do. While I'm locked up here, a prisoner for the Master, I want you to get out there and walk—better yet, run!—on the road God called you to travel. I don't want any of you sitting around on your hands. I don't want anyone strolling off, down some path that goes nowhere. And mark that you do this with humility and discipline—not in fits and starts, but steadily, pouring yourselves out for each other in acts of love, alert at noticing differences and quick at mending fences.

You were all called to travel on the same road and in the same direction, so stay together, both outwardly and inwardly. You have one Master, one faith, one baptism, one God and Father of all, who rules over all, works through all, and is present in all. Everything you are and think and do is permeated with Oneness. But that doesn't mean you should all look and speak and act the same.

Out of the generosity of Christ, each of us is given his own gift. The text for this is, He climbed the high mountain, He captured the enemy and seized the booty, He handed it all out in gifts to the people. It's true, is it not, that the One who climbed up also climbed down, down to the valley of earth? And the One who climbed down is the One who climbed back up, up to highest heaven. He handed out gifts above and below, filled heaven with his gifts, filled earth with his gifts.

He handed out gifts of apostle, prophet, evangelist, and pastor-teacher to train Christians in skilled servant work, working within Christ's body, the church, until we're all moving rhythmically and easily with each other, efficient and graceful in response to God's Son, fully mature adults, fully developed within and without, fully alive like Christ.

Ephesians 4:1–13 The Message

In the network of which we are a part, www.ReproducingChurches.com, we call our various groups across the network "CityGroups," describing the group so as to emphasize that they are leaders who want to love the city together. We call this concept City Church, emphasizing being the church together as one church to the city. While there may be many local expressions of His church in that city, just like there are many kinds of people living in that city, there is really only His church in that city. It's not a bunch of MY churches competing for the people of the city. Rather, it is a bunch of expressions of His church loving the people of the city for the sake of the mission of One Savior instead of the growth of one church.

{City Church}

Let's pause here for a minute just to process a few questions about beyond MY church thinking specifically with regard to City Church—living as followers of Jesus whom He prayed would be united on mission for the people of the city in which we live.

So, what is City Church exactly?

Short and sweet answer—every local expression of church in a given city giving themselves away together to cultivate the gospel throughout their city so that they might see "on earth as it is in heaven" there.

Why City Church?

:: *because the New Testament does not describe the church in terms of entity but rather in terms of evidence. Whereas, in America, we have defined church more by our doctrinal distinctives than we have by our common Savior and His commands to love. Because Jesus prayed for the unity of His followers.*

:: *because it is highly questionable for someone to go into a city and care nothing about what other followers of Jesus are already doing there before that someone arrived.*

:: *because based on what Jesus prayed (John 17:18–23) and based on what He commanded (John 13:34–35), our love for one another is what demonstrates that we know Jesus and live His ways.*

:: *because based on the ways that every epistle writer describes the church, our unity around the gospel is what compels us to see "on earth as it is in heaven" right here in our cities. An individualistic effort to "grow MY church" is nothing more than an attempt to build a personal following and often does not even point people to the One who was sent.*

How would living out City Church thinking impact the starting of new local church expressions and the refocusing of existing local church expressions for followers of Jesus, whether they are considered "clergy" or not?

Might I suggest three basic ways:

1) If a follower of Jesus thinks and lives beyond MY church with a City Church mindset, then he or she will not just start one church or help to renew one church. Rather, he or she will plant the gospel in their community, water it with love day after day after day, and watch God blossom "on earth as it is in heaven" in their family, on their street, in the marketplace, in local community, and around the world however He wants to grow His church.

2) He or she will not put all of his or her energy into growing one organization. Rather, he or she will think and live beyond just the activities and programs and needs of that one organization. He or she will think far beyond just inviting people to a Sunday gathering to hear a preacher preach. He or she will think about more than just getting people involved in a study. He or she will think about more than just filling volunteer gaps for church events. Instead, the one who thinks and lives in terms of City Church will not only personally cultivate the gospel in the everyday, regardless of whose local church expressions benefit from new believers and new members, but he or she will equip other people to plant the gospel in their spheres of influence with the same unified disregard for who benefits or gets credit.

3) *He or she will not be satisfied with simply starting one new local expression of the church or helping to renew one local church expression. Rather, he or she will think and live intentionally in setting strategy and setting goals such that beyond self living occurs in everything that happens and beyond MY church success is always the result. The focus will not be on the growth or success of one local church, but instead it will be on the advance of His church, alive in and among the city.*

How is City Church important/valuable in fulfilling the Great Commission?

I am not trying to sound like a simpleton here, but if I take the prayer Jesus prayed in John 17 seriously, then one cannot fulfill the Great Commission without thinking in terms of City Church. How could I assert that? Well, Jesus prayed in John 17:18–23 that His followers and those who would believe from their witness would be one with the Father just like Jesus was one with the Father. He prayed they would be consecrated for the work of God. Jesus defined the work of God in John 6:29—"that you believe in Him whom He has sent." In John 17, Jesus prayed for His followers to be consecrated in unity for the work of God, so that the world would know that the Father sent Him.

If I understand what Jesus is saying here correctly, and if I believe that fulfilling the Great Commission is synonymous with the "work of God," then I can only conclude that the Great Commission cannot be fulfilled without the unity of Jesus' followers around the work of God.

Without thinking and living in terms of City Church, therefore, I would suggest that the Great Commission will not be fulfilled in our city or around the world, period. We can pray for revival and a move of God all we want. But until we get to moving as His church together the way Jesus intended for us to move, as one, we will not be involved or see the work of God.

{some research}

My friend Dave helped me ask some church leaders two questions. One, on a scale of 1 to 10, 10 being high priority, how much of a priority is connection with other local churches to your overall strategy as a church? And two, what are you doing to grow in unity with the local churches around you? You should ask yourself and the other folks you walk with the same questions.

On the first question, I was surprised to see that the answers indicated about a 5 out of 10 when it came to the level of priority there was for unity among local church expressions. I confess that I thought it would be lower. However, while 85.7 percent of statistics are made up on the spot (not an original quote to me—think it was Ed Stetzer, the King of Church Statistics, who said it), these statistical findings were not made up. But I do think that because we used our social network for part of the research that some of the folks in the research group have sensed God calling them to prioritize unity and have done so. Thus, the fact that they participated in the survey may have skewed the data. But it may not have. There's a 43.9 percent chance that I am correct in my skewed assumptions.

On the second question, may I share with you some of the more common types of responses? Each one will be followed by a few of my personal thoughts on the matter. Mind you, this was a simply survey. My thoughts are simply based on their short responses. I don't know their full situation. Here are five of the more common responses.

1) RESPONSE:
"We meet with the local association of pastors once a month."

< my thoughts—If I were encouraging this person, I would ask a simple question—what are you doing tangibly that people in the community would observe and recognize as a unified effort to love and serve the city? I would ask this simply because our city will know we follow Jesus and are living His ways by our love (John 13:34–35) and because our maturity in unity will be a catalyst for them believing in the One who was sent (John 17:18–23). >

2) RESPONSE:
"We have made other churches aware of our activities and attempted to enlist them in community worship services."

< my thoughts—If I were encouraging this person, I would challenge them not to just make others aware of their own activities and scheduled worship services. I would challenge them to ask, "What are you doing that we could help with or support?" I would challenge them to approach the city leaders together asking for a specific way to serve the people of the city that would engage them in friendship and cultivate for unity in the city. I would challenge in this way simply because making someone aware of what you are doing is not cultivating for unity. >

3) RESPONSE:
"I am meeting with other pastors, planning combined events, uniting for training and outreach emphasis. The problem is going to occur in the large church/small church interaction. We have found that the local large churches 300 plus are doing

nothing to aid the smaller churches or build relationships. They are only interested in having my members come and join in what they are doing. That has happened a couple of times and I lost members both times. I no longer try to unify with churches larger than my own. It ends up a competition, and we always lose."

< my thoughts—My caution if I were encouraging this person would be that to say something like "we always lose" is an indication that you are not fully sold out to unity. Jesus "lost" a whole lot for our gain at the Cross, and yet He went through with it. >

4) RESPONSE:
"Nothing."

< my thoughts—The problem with this one is that in response to the first question, they said that unity among local church expressions in the city where they live is 8 out of 10 on the high priority scale. Eight out of 10 and they are not specifically doing anything to cultivate for unity among the local church expressions? >

5) RESPONSE:
"As a new church start I feel it is imperative we work in unity with other local churches of all Christian denominations. Some of the ways we are reaching out to our sister churches are as follows. I personally belong to a pastor's accountability group of three other pastors, one an Assemblies of God, one a Lutheran, and the other nondenominational. We meet once a week for lunch, where we encourage one another, share how our churches are involved in community, and discuss how we can partner with one another to further the kingdom. Another way we are connecting is through prayer. Each week during our large group

worship celebration we take time to pray specifically for one or two sister churches in our area. A card is sent to the pastor of the church with a short note letting them know we care about them and are praying for them, their members and ministries.

I attend the monthly Reproducing Churches Network meeting in Lakeland and have been able to network with others in the area. Those in attendance have been a great help to me personally during this time of starting a new work."

< my thoughts—This one obviously makes me smile for several reasons. I dig that this person is connecting on a deep level with other leaders in the city. The accountability group along with weekly lunch is so much more than so many others are doing to cultivate for unity. We need to be honest about the fact that we need to grow in relationship and trust with one another in order to grow in unity together, and this takes time together or it won't happen. I also dig that this person is a part of the CityGroup with the Reproducing Churches Network in Lakeland. I know those guys, and so this response is indicative of the fact that the CityGroup is effectively cultivating for unity and putting the interests of other local church expressions and other local leaders above their own. Not a lot of tangible action together yet, but with time and with this kind of cultivation, I would imagine that the trust and unity among these folks will blossom into something very like "on earth as it is in heaven" in the city where they live. >

{the church of west orange}

In early 2006, some of us here on the west side of Metro Orlando began to cultivate for unity among the local church expressions. It was not easy. A lot of coffees and lunches and conversations and assertions and dreams shared and rejections later. On December 10, 2008, a meeting occurred at House Blend Cafe in Ocoee, Florida, with a group of pastors from some of the churches across the West Orange County area. The purpose of the meeting was to discuss how we could be the church TOGETHER to the people of West Orange County (Orlando is in Orange County) and beyond.

We all agreed that beginning in 2009, we MUST forsake being territorial, being focused on "growing our own church," being concerned about the people of our cities coming to church buildings on Sunday mornings, and rather be focused to go and serve the people of West Orange County right where they are with attention to the needs that they are dealing with at the time.

We also talked about the importance of giving energy to the "overlooked and ignored." The "least of these" as Jesus described it in Matthew 25. Feeding the hungry. Clothing the naked. Giving water to the thirsty. Housing the homeless. Visiting the imprisoned. Not recreating the wheel. But rather more intensely supporting the various ministries already existing here, while creating new ones that would fill in the gaps.

It simply made sense to those of us who initially committed to think and live as one. One church with one Savior and one purpose—the same purpose Jesus had. To love God and to love people and to glorify His Father in heaven, living in oneness with the Father and living out the oneness of the Father's love in the everyday. His church with many expressions. The Church of West Orange was born—many local expressions being the church together to West Orange County and beyond.

We made one thing clear. Unity doesn't equal unanimity. Distinctives will continue to exist, but not as dividers. Rather as beautiful differences used in the midst of unity to be strengths that will sharpen all of us. Those distinctives exist in our gatherings and our various local expressions, but unified we can love and serve the people of West Orange County in ways that will show them Jesus, compassionately help them right now, and definitively shape the future of our community.

Here are a few of our stories.

Scott is a leader with Next Community Church in Winter Garden, Florida, a local church expression that is a part of the Church of West Orange that I mentioned in the previous chapter. He has led the Church of West Orange as a whole to serve the homeless together in our city through a fairly new ministry they helped create called Matthew's Hope. Among others things, they help offer timely and helpful services to the homeless in our community, from providing public IDs to healthcare to laundry service to showers to underwear to clothes to temporary shelter to counseling to job placement to shoes to meals to bike light kits.

That's right. Bike light kits. And get this. The local police even carry extra kits in their cars. If they see a homeless person riding a bike in the area at night without a light kit on it, instead of taking their bike and writing them up, they install a light kit on their bike. All because Scott and now more than 25 other church families have united together to love on our homeless friends in our community, and the local police have decided to help too.

Tom is also a part of the Church of West Orange. He leads Southwest Church. They gather in the local YMCA. He serves on the board with that local Y, and also serves the families of the Y in significant ways. In fact, not only does he serve the Y families, but he and the Southwest Church family together engage those YMCA families to serve alongside them multiple times a year. The projects vary from season to season and need to need, but they are engaging our city by providing them the opportunity to serve. We all pitch in together.

Mark is also a part of the Church of West Orange. He is an equipper with St. Paul's Presbyterian. He has a cool British accent too.

chapter eight

Mark and some of their crew had a dream of taking some of the very talented homeless musicians and recording their original songs. They sell the CDs and all proceeds are going to loving on the homeless of central Florida. You can purchase one at www.LoveRainsDown.com. And you should. Because it's good, heartfelt, and a result of the unity of the church and an example of the beautiful presence of God among us.

Chesta is with one of the local church expressions that associate with the Church of West Orange. She leads a ministry that she and her husband started that provides backpacks and school supplies to all the impoverished kids in the elementary and middle schools of West Orange County. Along with partnerships with local businesses, including Disney, and many local church expressions, they serve many families across the community. Many church families are working together, and many families are being blessed with supplies to meet their needs that they often can't afford. We all give into their efforts together.

Dale's family knows the tragedy of losing an unborn infant. His wife and daughters-in-law have suffered through miscarriages and still-births. It is an oft-ignored tragedy and due to the discomfort surrounding the subject, too often it is dealt with in a confusing and loss-for-words kind of way. Dale wanted to do something about that. He and his family, along with the Church of West Orange and other leaders in the area, are starting an unborn infant memorial. The groundbreaking was in October 2010. The memorial opened in May 2011. The goal is to provide a place and a support group for families struggling through the tangled web of emotions that come along with this significant loss. It also gives them the opportunity to group with others from across our city with whom they can grieve and heal and know the depth of near love. The website is www.UBAIM.com. Check it out. Dale united us all to serve a very tragic hurt in a large number of families in our community.

The Collins family, along with other families throughout the Church of West Orange, is a "safe family." Bethany Christian Services offers a program called Safe Families that works as a prevention concept with the foster care system. Families act as an intervention while Bethany Christian Services tries to help hurting parents before their kids are forced into the foster system. Families like the Collins open their home for a season to love on these beautiful kids. It is not easy at all. But they have told me often that it is worth it. I've looked into the eyes of the kids they have taken in. I can tell you it is well worth it. And I can tell you that it is a beautiful example of local church expressions emphasizing the importance of together helping kids in crisis.

John goes to jail a lot. But they let him out every time he does. He is loving on the prisoners of the 33rd Street Jail here in Orlando. You should hear the stories. He is not alone. Several leaders from several different local church expressions serve alongside him. It is a beautiful thing. Freedom in the midst of incarceration. The gospel alive among the prisoners. On earth as it is in heaven.

Cindy used to be on the streets herself. To hear her and her sister tell it, she wasn't anywhere near to being stable enough to give into the lives of hurting women just three years ago. But the near love of the living God changed all that. Now, Cindy gives herself away, with the support of several local church expressions, into the lives of women recovering from addiction and abuse. She leads S.A.S.H.A.'s Haven (a Safe And Sober Housing Alternative) here in our city, offering housing and mentoring to women who desperately need it. I have the privilege of looking into the eyes of these women usually once a week, and I can tell you that hope streams up from their healing hearts more and more each week that they are with Cindy. "On earth as it is in heaven" at its best.

chapter eight

Marcio and the students he leads, backed by many local leaders, have renovated many homes. Loretta, funded by several local church expressions, runs a local pregnancy center. Eric and Erin, simply because they care about their neighbors, consistently dine with and play with and care for the people who live directly around them. I could go on.

What's the point? The point is togetherness around mission. Unity for the sake of living sent together. Being of one heart and mind, as Jesus prayed in John 17, where He and His purposes are central—not me and my preferences.

Now please hear me. In no way do I want to hold up what we are cultivating for and living out together here in West Orange County as "having arrived" or the new model. On the contrary. I believe that we have a healthy story to share that may encourage you that unity can begin to be demonstrated among the local church expressions. However, I believe that we are only scratching the surface of unity here. In fact, just yesterday several of us were praying together and agreed that we are only now seeing the beginning of what unity could really look like among our local church expressions in our city. But we do believe it matters. We do believe that Jesus intended for His followers to unite in togetherness around His mission in order to love the people where we live in hopes of them believing in Him, the One who was sent.

{cultivating for unity among the local church expressions where you live}

Do you believe that too? If so, are you cultivating for unity among the local church expressions where you live? If not, then do you really believe it matters?

It is absolutely irrational to think that you will reap anything that you don't sow. The only exception, and it is why the gospel is so mysterious to our finite and linear thinking, is the grace given at the Cross when the wages of our sin were supernaturally transformed from death to life. We sowed for death. We now reap life in Christ, because he took upon himself the reaping of our sin. But that's the only exception. If we don't sow for unity, we won't reap it.

Jesus prayed for unity among His followers and wanted us to take it seriously. He now desires for us to sow selflessly for it—to deny self and take up our cross daily and follow Him. Consider these questions:

:: *Am I living "beyond MY church" to be the church together with other followers of Jesus in this city?*

:: *How will I cultivate for unity among the local church expressions in the community where I live—to join together with a vision for "on earth as it is in heaven" to happen in our city?*

:: *Will I do more than an occasional all-denominations worship gathering or yearly service project? Will I begin to consider the other local church expressions of our city as more important than "MY church"?*

Three points to consider as you think about those questions.

1) We must be willing to change our scorecard (as Missional Leadership Specialist Reggie McNeal says).
We know good and well that the success of the church in a city is not about "butts, buildings, and budgets." We know good and well that how many people gather, how often we have a building campaign, and whether we meet our budget are not necessarily God's way of measuring our effectiveness as His church. If we know this so good and well, then

why do so many people keep thinking and acting like this is the scorecard? Why do we focus on the success of MY church in these areas, rather than on the blossoming of "on earth as it is in heaven" on the streets and in the alleyways and in the homes and in the marketplaces of our city?

If we want to cultivate for unity, then we had better change our scorecard. Or else we will be so busy focusing on butts, buildings, and budgets that we will miss how God might want to blossom His church in our city beyond MY church.

Side note—I hear church leaders complain about people who "church swap." People who already follow Jesus that have a pattern of just swapping local church expressions for whatever is the latest and greatest at the time. Well, may I challenge any pastor reading this book? I think the onus is on us. If we will quit bowing to the idol of MY church having more people, more buildings, and a bigger budget, treating this like a product to be consumed, then maybe people will quit just consuming a product and start being the church in our cities. Just saying.

2) *We must be willing to do whatever it takes to be of one heart and mind with other followers of Jesus in the city where we live.*
Whatever it takes. Even if it means surrendering your own way of thinking about "church" and the success of "MY church." Even if it means someone else's local church expression appears to be more "successful" than the one of which you are a part. Even if it means that who gets the credit for stuff becomes secondary to the revealed presence of the living God. Even if it means that some of the common events or programs or focuses take a back seat to what God is doing in and among His church uniting together. Even if it means that you don't get to hear your favorite preacher every week or that you don't get the most exciting musical worship experience every week or that you have to coach your kids through difficult or uncertain or unsheltered situations. Even if it means the dissolution of any one entity for the sake of the evidence of His church in the city where you live.

The people from those stories I shared don't care what local church expression gets the credit for all this stuff they are doing or what local expression might benefit either. They aren't just doing random community service, but are instead simply meeting needs while making new friends in hopes of making disciples in the process—regardless of what local church expression those new followers connect with. And, they all sincerely hope for "on earth as it is in heaven" (the evidence of God's near love through the nearness of His united local church) to happen in our city, which will only happen when the various local expressions of His church move beyond MY church thinking and living toward being ONE church to the glory of God.

Side note—we need to understand, even beg God for wisdom, about what unity really is and what unity really isn't. And we need to realize that unity only occurs for followers of Jesus when what matters most to Him begins to matter most to us and when His way of thinking about His church becomes superior to any ways that we think about church. Oneness will come when we are of one mind and heart with regard to the things that are priority to the One who sent us to be His church in the first place.

3) We must begin to ask very honest and practical questions of God and of one another with regard to what unity in the city where we live might look like. Then we must be willing to do what He says.

The church in the New Testament is referred to by the evidence of the church in a city not by the entities of the church in a city. Earlier in the book, we established this idea and argued for it. At the risk of being redundant, let me just offer this reminder: MY church is not "MY" church anyway. To try to cultivate for transformation in our city alone, apart from the amazing giftedness and strengths of other local church expressions,

chapter eight

would be foolish as well as in complete contradiction to the prayer Jesus prayed in the Garden in John 17. TOGETHER our compassion will be the demonstration of the nearness of God. And others will believe in the One who was sent as they see us unite around His unconditional love, live out His unending mission, and plant and water His love so that His kingdom blossoms in and around our city.

Now, with that reminder, I suggest that to pray for and talk about unity is one thing. To begin to live it out together is altogether different. We must do both. And we must ask honest questions that may hurt and may even cause heated discussion. But only as we walk through the refining fire of selfless relationship together will we become one.

We also have to ask very practical questions. How will we support and encourage and pray for what each local expression of the church in our city is doing? What are a few things we can begin to do together to cultivate unity? How do we talk about the importance of unity to other followers and make sense of what we are attempting ("People will only do what makes sense to them."—Harold Bullock). What would actual unity look like—the end result—if it really happened, and what would we need to sow to get there?

This is much more than what we have typically done. Much more than an occasional worship gathering all together. Much more than a Christmas lighting of the candles together. Much more than an Easter egg hunt together. Much more than a yearly or twice a year service project. This is about truly being the church together, His church, in our city and for our city.

In your city, I want to encourage you to:

:: **begin to get together with other followers of Jesus simply to pray for unity.**

:: **as you are praying and growing in relationship and trust with** *each other, begin to ask what the first steps toward unity might look like. Then, take them.*

:: *articulate a vision for unity in the city where you live so that you can share it with each local church expression and begin to act on it together.*

:: *pray for the desire for "on earth as it is in heaven" in the city more than for the growth of "MY church."*

:: *live in the everyday as His church committed to His mission to cultivate His gospel and water it with His love so that He can grow His church however He wants to in the city where He placed you.*

If you will, you will see how the evidence of the gospel comes alive in the city where you live. The church will be more than some local entity that has a building on a corner. You might begin to see Jesus in the eyes of the people you serve. You might begin to cheer when other followers of Jesus "succeed" on mission. You might begin to see God reveal Himself in ways that you have never seen. You might see a city transformed. You might see new evidences of the kingdom of God blossom. You might see "on earth as it is in heaven." All because His church is taking seriously what He prayed and living out what He commanded.

{the bottom line}

As local church expressions in the cities where we live, we must begin to take seriously what Jesus prayed for His followers and what He intended for His church. We must quit thinking of "church" as a business that we grow and make successful. We must think of her (His bride) instead as a glimpse of heaven on earth lived out and about in the midst of the people of our cities.

chapter eight

May we think and live "beyond MY church" as local expressions of His church together in and for our city.

CONSIDER and CONVERSE:

1. If the church were fully alive in the city where we live, what would that look like? Describe it in detail.

2. What do you think of the City Church concept and how might that kind of thinking and living change the way we think and live as the church in and for our city?

3. On a scale of 1 to 10, with 10 being high priority, how much of a priority is connection with other local churches to our overall strategy as a church? And, what are we doing to grow in unity with the local church expressions around us?

4. Are we willing to do whatever it would take to be of one heart and mind as followers of Jesus together in and for our city?

5. What do we think of the unity questions suggested in the end of this chapter? How will we (and who will go) to cultivate for unity among the local church expressions of our city such that we become His church in and for our city?

chapter 9

thinking and living beyond MY church to the world

She was a waitress at a Waffle House. You can probably smell it as soon as I mention it. The aroma of waffles rising, eggs being scrambled, toast being crisped, orange juice being poured, grease. Waffle House is a wonderful thing. Might kill you, but a wonderful thing.

My friend Derek and I were just sitting there talking. We had been kind to her, at least I think we had. Maybe we hadn't been kind, but I always try to be to waiters and waitresses. Maybe we were and that's why she felt comfortable enough to engage in conversation with us. But whatever it was, boy, did she engage!

She leaned in after a refill of my sweet tea and blurted out, "I used to believe in God. But I just can't any more. All because of the church. When my family and I were walking through hard times, they abandoned us. And they have abandoned the hurting people of this world too."

Her declaration made it clear that she had been wounded. Her tone made it clear that she was not interested in being convinced otherwise. She went on to tell us that she didn't hear or see God in our world any more. And she didn't understand the people who said they did see Him.

This is not just some disgruntled human created by the God she was resenting. This is a person hoping that she's wrong but disbelieving because of the representatives of God she resents. The picture of who God really is has not been pieced together for her, or maybe whatever supposed church group it was that wounded her just put the puzzle together wrong such that the image was horrific more than healing.

{the church—the puzzle of God to the world in this age}

Let's imagine His church in this age since the Cross and the Resurrection being the picture God wants to show about Himself and His ways to the world. The church is the puzzle of God to the world in this age. She is a picture of the relationship of oneness that He desires with the people that He made (at least in ideal form). Paul wrote in Ephesians 5:25

(NASB), "Husbands, love your wives, just as Christ also loved the church and gave Himself up for her." Many local church expressions coming together into one big wedding album picture in puzzle form providing an image of the unconditional, faithful, vowed, never-ending love of the Groom that is our God.

What section of the puzzle of His church is your local expression being? Are you bringing horrific images to our world, or are you demonstrating the near and healing image of God to a dark and hurting world?

On one hand, the church, especially the American church, certainly is puzzling to our world. I have spoken to people who would admit that they are not followers of Jesus who say they might believe in Jesus if the church would act like Him. You have probably heard this too. And who can blame them? They see the local church expressions of their city make claims about loving God and loving people, but then they see them spend millions on themselves while children in their city go hungry and orphans around the world go without parents. This certainly is puzzling, isn't it?

On the other hand, with so many pieces to this puzzle called "church" and with so many local church expressions, no wonder it is difficult for the world to see the full picture of the bride of Christ who ultimately lives for the glory of the Groom. Each local church expression represents a section of this puzzle. Each one represents the voice of God, or better said with regard to this metaphor, a God sighting. Each one offers a picture of the near love of God, an image of the One who made us in His image.

Depending upon the puzzle, depending upon how all those pieces come together, the world will either see the revealed presence of the living, loving God, or they will see a clouded image of Him. Clouded by our selfishness. Clouded by our divisiveness. Clouded by our disunity.

Depending upon how all these local church expressions fit together into this beautiful puzzle picturing Jesus' bride, the world will either believe in the One who was sent or they won't. At least that's what Jesus implies in His prayer in John 17.

It begs the question, then, in the midst of all the loneliness and woundedness and oppressiveness and sickness of our world, what would the puzzle look like to our world when all pieced together?

May I suggest at least three segments of what would have to be pictured here in our world in order for our world to see the nearness and the goodness of the Father represented through the image that is His church?

{love = THE PIECES}

When I put together the 63-piece Cinderella puzzle with Abby and Ella that they thoroughly enjoy, we do what all puzzle-putter-togetherers do. We lay out the pieces face up, grouping the ones with straight edges together and grouping the ones with jagged edges together. Then we begin to put the puzzle together.

Well, as we process this metaphor of the church being the puzzle of God to the world in this age, let's imagine the many pieces being LOVE. God's near love, His picture of love that He is sending one piece at a time into the lives of the people of our world. To the spouse. To the neighbor. To the co-worker. To the homeless man. To the orphan child. To the sex-trafficked girl. To the diseased. To the imprisoned. To the thirsty. To the hungry. To each of us through each of us who call ourselves followers of the One who was sent to display God's light in the darkness. And He is the best image of God anyone has ever seen, as Eugene Peterson puts it in *The Message*:

All they have eyes for is the fashionable god of darkness. They think he can give them what they want, and that they won't have to bother believing a Truth they

can't see. They're stone-blind to the dayspring brightness of the Message that shines with Christ, who gives us the best picture of God we'll ever get.
2 Corinthians 4:4 The Message

In the context of this verse in 2 Corinthians, Paul was writing about how we as the church are the letters of His love, the displayers of the Truth, the clay pots that contain the unbreakable power of the living, loving God. We are the puzzle picture now following the One who was the best picture of God we'll ever get.

And Jesus gave us specific instructions as to what piece of the puzzle He most wanted us to be. He laid out the pieces. Each of them different. Some jagged and some straight-edged. Some simple and some multifaceted. But all segments of His love. Because it is our love for one another and for the people of our world that will demonstrate the ways of the One we follow more than anything else.

"Let me give you a new command: Love one another. In the same way I loved you, you love one another. This is how everyone will recognize that you are my disciples—when they see the love you have for each other."
John 13:34–35 The Message

It begs the question—how has Jesus loved us? He said in these verses that we are to love "in the same way I loved you." So, how has He loved us?

At the risk of being labeled as a simpleton, I would suggest that He has loved us by laying His life down and holding our interests up.

This is how we've come to understand and experience love: Christ sacrificed his life for us. This is why we ought to live sacrificially for our fellow believers, and not just be out for ourselves.
1 John 3:16 The Message

Therefore if there is any encouragement in Christ, if there is any consolation of

love, if there is any fellowship of the Spirit, if any affection and compassion, make my joy complete by being of the same mind, maintaining the same love, united in spirit, intent on one purpose. Do nothing from selfishness or empty conceit, but with humility of mind regard one another as more important than yourselves; do not merely look out for your own personal interests, but also for the interests of others.
Philippians 2:1–4 NASB

When we give our lives away for the sake of others having life, and when we think of the interests of others before we think of our own interests, then and only then are we loving like Jesus loved. This is not a warm, fuzzy kind of love. This is a no-way-I-can-do-this-without-denying-myself kind of love. This is a no-way-I-can-do-this-without-His-Spirit-blossoming-His-love-out-of-me kind of love.

In order to love like this, in order to be the puzzle piece of love He intended and commanded us to be, all of us are going to have to be cured of one epidemic disease that plagues church culture. I call it "churchmustfeedmeitis." All of us are going to have to think and live for the sake of what we give as the church, rather than thinking and living for what we get out of church.

It is hard to swallow I know. It is a big horse pill. The elephant in the room, so to speak. One bite at a time, as they say, will be required to swallow it. But we must if we want to be cured. If we want to love like Jesus loved.

What if we didn't have a light system and a fog machine that might make our worship gathering a more engaging environment, and instead used that $100,000 for a home for hurting women? What if we thought less about the quality of the music on Sunday mornings and more about singing songs to Jesus with a once-lonely widow who has now become a friend? What if our students didn't pay $400 for a week of camp-high experience and instead bought groceries for a hungry family from their high school that they delivered themselves and maybe even cooked and dined with them? What if we worried less about a well-kept church building and thought more about how the people of our community might be able to use it to serve their wants and needs? What if we spent less on cooler toys for our kids' ministry and gave more to a family trying to adopt a child without a home? What if when we strategized about future vision we asked city leaders what they wanted most in our city for the future before we even considered our own dreams?

Sounds radical? Maybe. Maybe not. Maybe it just sounds loving.

And maybe if the very diverse pieces of the puzzle that is His church, the many local expressions, united together to love the city and the world like this then maybe, just maybe, the world would know and believe in the One who was sent.

{reconciliation = PUTTING THE PIECES TOGETHER}

I am normally not a very dogmatic person. At least not just about my speculative opinions. But I am going to assert something here that I believe to be correct because it seems to me that the Scriptures declare it so. Here goes.

If reconciliation, the healing of broken and divided relationships, *is not happening in your own relationships*, in your own family and among the church family of which you are a part and at work and among your neighbors and in the city where you live, *then the gospel is something you may talk about but don't live out.*

I would suggest that nowhere in all of Scripture is the picture of what God intended for His church and even for all of humanity described more clearly than in 2 Corinthians 5:17–21. Nowhere else in Scripture, in my opinion, is the gospel described with such distinct imagery than in these verses. Take a look:

Now we look inside, and what we see is that anyone united with the Messiah gets a fresh start, is created new. The old life is gone; a new life burgeons! Look at

it! All this comes from the God who settled the relationship between us and him, and then called us to settle our relationships with each other. God put the world square with himself through the Messiah, giving the world a fresh start by offering forgiveness of sins. God has given us the task of telling everyone what he is doing. We're Christ's representatives. God uses us to persuade men and women to drop their differences and enter into God's work of making things right between them. We're speaking for Christ himself now: Become friends with God; he's already a friend with you. How? you ask. In Christ. God put the wrong on him who never did anything wrong, so we could be put right with God.
2 Corinthians 5:17–21 The Message

In the context of these verses, Paul was asserting the necessity of the followers in Corinth to both get along with each other as well as be letters of God's love to the people of that diverse city. He described God as the worker of reconciliation and, just like John in First John, Paul asserts that our reconciliation with God will show itself in the way we reconcile with one another. The puzzle, when the pieces of love come together, will be a picture of reconciliation such that only a holy, selfless God could create through a people fully surrendered to Him.

When the gospel of Jesus has taken root and blossomed in my life and in the lives of the other followers of Jesus with whom I walk, then at least some evidence of budding reconciliation—if not full-blown restored relationships—will be seen in and among my relationships.

If this is the case, why do I pretend that the gospel is something that makes me look perfect, rather than something that inspires and enables me to perfectly love? If this is the case, why are we satisfied with contention rather than unity in and among the local church expressions of our city? If this is the case, why do we stand idly by while hateful segregation remains both through racial boundaries as well as socioeconomic divides? These are not the real evidences of the gospel!

The evidence of the gospel is not seen when families pretend like they have it all together. The evidence of the gospel is seen when families who don't have it all together are transformed to begin to grow together. The evidence of the gospel is not seen when people pretend that they don't lie, steal, or hurt others. The evidence of the gospel is seen when people who did lie and steal and hurt others begin to tell the truth, serve, and love others. The evidence of the gospel is not seen when a rich group helps a poor group in a service project or when a white group helps a black group with a community project. The evidence of the gospel is seen when the rich and poor and black and white have relationships beyond just a few days of community service projects. The church is fully alive in a city, not when there are religious rituals on Sundays but rather when there is evidence of reconciled relationships every day.

Maybe if the very diverse pieces of the puzzle that is His church, the many local expressions, were put together and a picture of reconciliation resulted in our families and local church families and in our cities, then maybe, just maybe, the world would know and believe in the One who was sent.

{unity = PUZZLE PICTURE THAT IS MADE}

We arrive once again at the place where we must grapple with Jesus' prayer in John 17. We as His supposed followers must decide whether we will take seriously what He prayed in John 17 and live it out by His enabling strength and transforming power, or whether we will live complacent and misguided and off mission in disunity.

In the same way that you gave me a mission in the world, I give them a mission in the world. I'm consecrating myself for their sakes so they'll be truth-consecrated in their mission. I'm praying not only for them but also for those who will believe in me because of them and their witness about me. The goal is for all of them to become one heart and mind—just as you, Father, are in me and I in you, so they might be one heart and mind with us. Then the world might believe that you, in fact, sent me. The same glory you gave me, I gave them, so they'll be as unified and together

as we are—I in them and you in me. Then they'll be mature in this oneness, and give the godless world evidence that you've sent me and loved them in the same way you've loved me.
John 17:18–23 The Message

This mission for which the consecrated One has consecrated us, this one heart and mind that is a priority so that the work of God may occur, this maturity of unity that will validate the One who was sent, is of utmost importance. It is worth surrendering anything we must surrender. It is worth suffering anything we must suffer. It is worth dying for, especially if it means that the death of holding my interests in life so dearly will result in life abundant coming to those who are currently dying in woundedness and loneliness and sickness and oppressiveness and darkness without Christ.

Unity *is not* doing a few things together as local church expressions. Rather, it is committing together to engage our city on a mission of love with a must-be-heard-and-seen gospel for the sake of a population of people whose survival matters more than the survival of our individual church expressions.

My friend recently told me that he has a friend who became a Navy SEAL. This new warrior extraordinaire relayed the story of the final week of cuts to his friend. That final week when the field of candidates is narrowed drastically and the actual SEALS are chosen. It is a week when those who already think and act like a Navy SEAL get to become one. Why did he put it in those terms? Because in that final week, the drills and exercises are so strict and rigorous that those in command are able to discern who cares only about their own survival in contrast to those who care about the survival of others above their own. Because when those warriors find themselves in the midst of the most threatening, heated mission they will ever face, not one person on that team will chicken out or freak out or choose their own survival over the accomplishment of the mission at hand.

chapter nine

Does the mission of the Navy SEAL matter more than the mission of the church? More specifically, doesn't that same principle apply to His church? The mission for which we have been consecrated matters much more than do the individual goals that we set for our respective local church expressions. And so do the lives of those who are lost without the hope of Christ.

We need to wake up from our divided slumber. We need to quit letting our own preferred interests and our own dear doctrines and our self-proclaimed successful methods divide us and disable us from accomplishing the mission for which we have been consecrated.

The unity of the church is not seen in common interests, doctrine, or methods. The unity of the church is seen most in the commitment that the followers of Jesus within a city have to demonstrate the unconditional love of Jesus to that city through their love for one another and their obedience to learn and live the ways of Jesus in and among the people of their city as they make disciples there.

Unity means that we think and live and move in our everyday listening to the same Leader, driven by the same purpose, focused on the same outcome. And you don't keep score of who did this or who did that or who served in this way or who served in that way. You never say, "Look what we did."

You instead declare, "Look what He did." You don't stand up at the end of a unified effort and say, "Look at the puzzle MY church put together." You stand up and say, "Look at the picture of God that He has put on display through the love that He has blossomed in us!"

{the bottom line}

If you are truly committed to the mission to take the love of God (who so loved the world He gave His only Son) into all the world, then there will be evidence of the church existing in our world besides just in buildings on a corner and gatherings on Sunday morning and Wednesday nights and meetings where you get together to sing and hear a teacher. There will be the revealed presence of God as He has chosen to reveal it—through love, through reconciliation, and through unity.

The image of the One who made us will be the final picture seen when the puzzle pieces of His local church expressions unite to be His church together for the glory of God unto all the world.

CONSIDER and CONVERSE:

1. Do we know people who are disgusted with God or with the church? Why are they so disgusted?

2. What is the picture of God that the people of the city where we live are seeing as they look at all the local church expressions here?

3. Are we loving one another, loving the other local church expressions, and loving the people of our city the way that Jesus loves us?

4. How much does unity matter to us? Are we willing to sow whatever it will take to reap unity among the local church expressions of our city?

5. Is there evidence of reconciliation in our relationships, or could people doubt the living presence of the gospel in our relationships?

chapter 10

moving beyond MY to HIS and
US from here on out

When do you know if a local church expression has been "successful" and effective?

I have asked this of many groups of leaders over the last three or four years, and the answers are varied. From more people to more buildings to more baptisms, the answers unfortunately usually center on that local church expression rather than on the mission of God and "on earth as it is in heaven" happening in the city where that local church expression is being the church. And rarely, I mean almost never, has the word unity come up.

How have we missed this? How have we missed what Jesus prayed for in the Garden? How have we missed what love really is and what love really does and what love really causes? How have we missed that Jesus did not die for the success of the entity of the church but rather in order to transform the self-absorbed reality of "on earth" into the beyond-self beauty of "heaven" right here and right now in our cities.

John Frame in his book *Evangelical Reunion* asserts:

"God's sovereignty is not opposed to human responsibility. Rather, the former undergirds the latter. We are encouraged to seek God's kingdom because we know that God is bringing His kingdom to the earth. We also know that God's sovereign plan regularly makes use of human agents to accomplish divine goals. So it is evident that God wishes us to do what we can to rid the church of its divisions."

God did not intend for there to be disunity in His church any more than He intended for there to be disunity in the Garden of Eden. And God's restoration effect, or in other words the incarnational presence of His gospel alive in our everyday, was not limited to individuals like those from the Garden of Eden, but rather was intended to show the effect of restoration among the supposed followers of Jesus as a whole too. Furthermore, God wants us to deny ourselves and take up our cross daily

chapter ten

not only for our personal growth but also for the sake of that picture of oneness with Him that He calls His bride, His church.

Dietrich Bonhoeffer is quoted as having said, "The church is only the church when it exists for others." My only slight alteration to his wonderful statement would be to choose the pronoun "she" in lieu of "it," but that is simply to emphasize that the church is people who were intended to exist to give themselves away into one another and into our world.

Kind of like the folks in Macedonia. Paul boldly mentioned their unity and generosity in a very direct contrast to the divisiveness of the folks in Corinth. Check this out:

Now, friends, I want to report on the surprising and generous ways in which God is working in the churches in Macedonia province. Fierce troubles came down on the people of those churches, pushing them to the very limit. The trial exposed their true colors: They were incredibly happy, though desperately poor. The pressure triggered something totally unexpected: an outpouring of pure and generous gifts. I was there and saw it for myself. They gave offerings of whatever they could—far more than they could afford!—pleading for the privilege of helping out in the relief of poor Christians. This was totally spontaneous, entirely their own idea, and caught us completely off guard. What explains it was that they had first given themselves unreservedly to God and to us. The other giving simply flowed out of the purposes of God working in their lives.
2 Corinthians 8:1–5 The Message

They didn't give generously because they ought to. They gave because they were compelled to. The interests-of-others-above-my-own kind of love that had been poured out for them in Christ not only saved them but it kept shaping them day after day after day.

Instead of focusing on living *for* God, competing for personal position, striving to be viewed as better than anyone else, and pretending to have it all, like Corinth, maybe we today need to focus on living *with* God, compelled to put the interests of other followers of Jesus and local church expressions above our own, living to love, and demonstrating a poverty made abundant by Christ's love, like Macedonia.

Wouldn't the world notice that? Don't you think the world would know and believe in the One who was sent if they saw His supposed followers living like Him? Wouldn't this be the way to represent Him as His ambassadors (2 Corinthians 5)?

But what would have to happen, particularly in American church culture, for this unity thing to happen? I need to admit to you that my study of Jesus' prayer in John 17 over the last five years has wrecked me. And I need to admit to you that what we would have to sow to "rid the church of its divisions" (as Frame wrote) and what would have to fall away into trash piles of human effort rather than God's intent are difficult to put my mind around. In fact, it just plain scares me to death.

However, it also scares me to life. Better said, to live. To live changed by the gospel of grace, now compelled to give away gracious love. My goodness superseded by the goodness of God displayed by the unity of those He called His body and His bride. His mission superior to any of MY church's word-smithed mission statements. Focused on what others, whether lost or found, are becoming rather than on what I am attempting to become.

{the "what ifs" of moving beyond MY to HIS and US}

So what are some of the possible implications from here on out if we dropped the MY church thinking and living and began to be the church together in our cities in ways that demonstrate we are His church and that our unity matters because of its impact on the mission and work of God? Rather than attempting to predict actual occurrences, please permit me to ask some rhetorical "what if" questions that we can process together. These are simply my suggestions of what we might have to move beyond in order to think and live HIS and US and THEM from here on out.

1) beyond MY name to HIS name alone
What if we even dropped our names and labels and began to operate less like separate, competing entities and instead simply lived for His name's sake?

2) beyond MY credit to HIS glory
What if we planted the gospel and watered it with love in our families, our neighborhoods, our marketplaces, our cities, our world, and on the Web? And then what if we didn't care what local church expression benefited as long as God revealed Himself and lives were changed and people were making disciples, learning and living His ways with others?

"The true measure of a man is how he treats someone who can do him absolutely no good."
(Samuel Johnson, eighteenth-century British author)

3) beyond MY financial stability to HIS provision toward an US effort
What if we quit worrying about individual accumulation and stable retirement and focused our resources toward the greatest needs in each other's lives and toward the greatest impact in our cities?

4) beyond MY salaries to HIS daily bread
What if we quit setting salaries for pastors and equippers based on corporate standards and began to appreciate them with whatever it took to show gratefulness and provide the daily bread their families need?

5) beyond MY church consumerism toward a THEM generosity
What if we prayed for church leaders to know and to be assured that we want to be equipped rather than fed, that we want to give ourselves away as the church rather than be consumers who get more and more out of church?

6) beyond MY church preservation toward a THEM restoration

What if we quit setting up church budgets to preserve what we have and instead directed them to give like His riches are limitless for the sake of the restoration of lives, even if it meant we may die bouncing our last check (as some theologian is quoted to have said)?

7) beyond MY measurements to HIS fruitfulness

What if we quit defining success in terms of "taking it to the next level" with regard to budgets and buildings, and instead equipped and challenged people to be making next-level disciples who make next-level disciples who make next-level disciples and so on?

8) beyond "attending MY church" toward an US community

What if we introduced neighbors (who live in close proximity to one another) from each of our local church expressions, asked them to exchange contact info, challenged them to connect consistently? What if we freed them from unnecessary scheduled church events, got them to serve their other neighbors together, resourced them to serve together one way locally with their neighbors, encouraged them to serve together one way globally with their neighbors, and maybe even equipped them to study the Scriptures together? Would that be enough evidence of "church" for us, or would that not be "entity" enough?

"Get involved in situations such as neighborhood Bible studies and chaplaincies where you are forced to share fellowship and/or ministry with Christians from other traditions. Allow the sense of unity you gain from such experiences to color your view of the church."
(John Frame, *Evangelical Reunion*)

9) beyond MY church's interests toward success of HIS other expressions

What if every local church expression woke up every morning of every day thinking more about the interests and activities of other local church expressions so much so that each of us would be taken care of because we are thinking so much of one another and so much so that even if the local church expression of which you are a part dissolves the kingdom overall gains?

10) beyond MY doctrinal divides toward our differences sharpening US

What if we considered our doctrinal differences not to be divides as much as they are opportunities for conversation and sharpening, and what if we realized that some of our doctrines that we hold dear that cause division aren't as important to Jesus as we might think they are?

"Seek involvement of other denominations when there are doctrinal disputes in your own. Seek to turn doctrinal debates into occasions for the whole church, or as much of it as possible, to study together."
(John Frame, *Evangelical Reunion*)

11) beyond MY gathering toward HIS mission daily for THEM

What if we quit thinking of gathering as the ultimate experience and instead considered worship gatherings as catalysts for mission, gathering so that we come to celebrate God's mission and then leave to live sent daily in HIS mission, offering glimpses of "on earth as it is in heaven" smack dab in the middle of our culture through our love for one another and our love for the people of our cities?

12) beyond MY generation's preservation and preferences toward HIS next generation's restoration and unity

What if we prayed to be so changed from our MY church thinking and living to live as HIS church united on mission, such that the next generation couldn't help but develop a new view of "church," would quit only being converted to "go to church" on Sundays, and would be united and compelled to "be the church" daily?

{requirement to think and live beyond MY church—TRUST}

One principle that definitely has been a thread through this book, whether directly or indirectly, is the trust it would take to think and live "beyond MY church." We would have to grow not only in our trust for one another as followers of Jesus together on mission in our city and for our city, but we would also have to grow to trust that God will take care of each and every one of our needs, our actual needs (not our wants), if we surrender to fully live as HIS church as He prayed and intended.

It will stretch us, no doubt. The potential of what could happen may look unlike anything we have ever seen, especially here in America. But whether we are willing to think and live "beyond MY church" is a real evidence of just how much we say we trust God as opposed to just how much we trust Him. If we aren't willing to go there, it is probably because of fear. Fear of not surviving if we become too generous. Fear of not "growing MY church" if we highlight and support what too many other local church expressions are doing. Fear of somebody teaching the wrong doctrine and not having the ability to do "truth patrol" for "MY church" if we relate too much together with other local church expressions. Fear of God may be not having the riches He says He has and may be that He won't keep the promises that He said He'd keep.

It may be worth being reminded of these four Scriptures that have in some way been shared in this book. Please reread them here, meditate on them, and ask God to grow each of us to trust Him enough to think and live "beyond MY church" as He intended.

{think on and live out these things, with His help}

In the same way that you gave me a mission in the world, I give them a mission in the world. I'm consecrating myself for their sakes so they'll be truth-consecrated in

their mission. I'm praying not only for them but also for those who will believe in me because of them and their witness about me. The goal is for all of them to become one heart and mind—just as you, Father, are in me and I in you, so they might be one heart and mind with us. Then the world might believe that you, in fact, sent me. The same glory you gave me, I gave them, so they'll be as unified and together as we are—I in them and you in me. Then they'll be mature in this oneness, and give the godless world evidence that you've sent me and loved them in the same way you've loved me.
John 17:18–23 The Message

Shout! A full-throated shout! Hold nothing back-a trumpet-blast shout! Tell my people what's wrong with their lives, face my family Jacob with their sins! They're busy, busy, busy at worship, and love studying all about me. To all appearances they're a nation of right-living people-law-abiding, God-honoring. They ask me, "What's the right thing to do?" and love having me on their side. But they also complain, "Why do we fast and you don't look our way? Why do we humble ourselves and you don't even notice?"

Well, here's why: The bottom line on your "fast days" is profit. You drive your employees much too hard. You fast, but at the same time you bicker and fight. You fast, but you swing a mean fist. The kind of fasting you do won't get your prayers off the ground. Do you think this is the kind of fast day I'm after: a day to show off humility? To put on a pious long face and parade around solemnly in black? Do you call that fasting, a fast day that I, God, would like?

This is the kind of fast day I'm after: to break the chains of injustice, get rid of exploitation in the workplace, free the oppressed, cancel debts. What I'm interested in seeing you do is: sharing your food with the hungry, inviting the homeless poor into your homes, putting clothes on the shivering ill-clad, being available to your own families. Do this and the lights will turn on, and your lives will turn around at once. Your righteousness will pave your way. The God of glory will secure your passage. Then when you pray, God will answer. You'll call out for help and I'll say, "Here I am."

If you get rid of unfair practices, quit blaming victims, quit gossiping about other

people's sins, if you are generous with the hungry and start giving yourselves to the down-and-out, your lives will begin to glow in the darkness, your shadowed lives will be bathed in sunlight. I will always show you where to go. I'll give you a full life in the emptiest of places—firm muscles, strong bones. You'll be like a well-watered garden, a gurgling spring that never runs dry.
Isaiah 58:1-11 The Message

And my God will supply all your needs according to His riches in glory in Christ Jesus.
Philippians 4:19 NASB

"If your first concern is to look after yourself, you'll never find yourself. But if you forget about yourself and look to me, you'll find both yourself and me. We are intimately linked in this harvest work. Anyone who accepts what you do, accepts me, the One who sent you. Anyone who accepts what I do accepts my Father, who sent me. Accepting a messenger of God is as good as being God's messenger. Accepting someone's help is as good as giving someone help. This is a large work I've called you into, but don't be overwhelmed by it. It's best to start small. Give a cool cup of water to someone who is thirsty, for instance. The smallest act of giving or receiving makes you a true apprentice. You won't lose out on a thing."
Matthew 10:39-42 The Message

{the bottom line}

What would it take to move from MY church thinking and living to HIS church and OUR unity thinking and living?

When you get together as followers of Jesus and talk about it, what would have to be emphasized? What would be some first steps?

What would have to be let go? What might it look like?

How might our city and our world be changed?

How many new local expressions of the church might blossom up across our cities? How many existing local church expressions might be renewed and reinvigorated?

How might the widow and orphan and sick and hungry and thirsty and lonely and oppressed and exploited be cared for?

How might we, if we actually think and live beyond MY church together, experience His love and know what He originally intended for us?

May we think and live beyond MY church so that the world will know and believe in the One who was sent.

CONSIDER and CONVERSE:

Take the questions offered in "the bottom line" of this last chapter and spend several months meeting about and conversing about these. Then set some next steps, some "what will we sow first?" kind of actions. Then just listen and obey, knowing that you are doing what God Himself prayed for, confident that a product of unity will be people knowing and believing in the One who was sent.

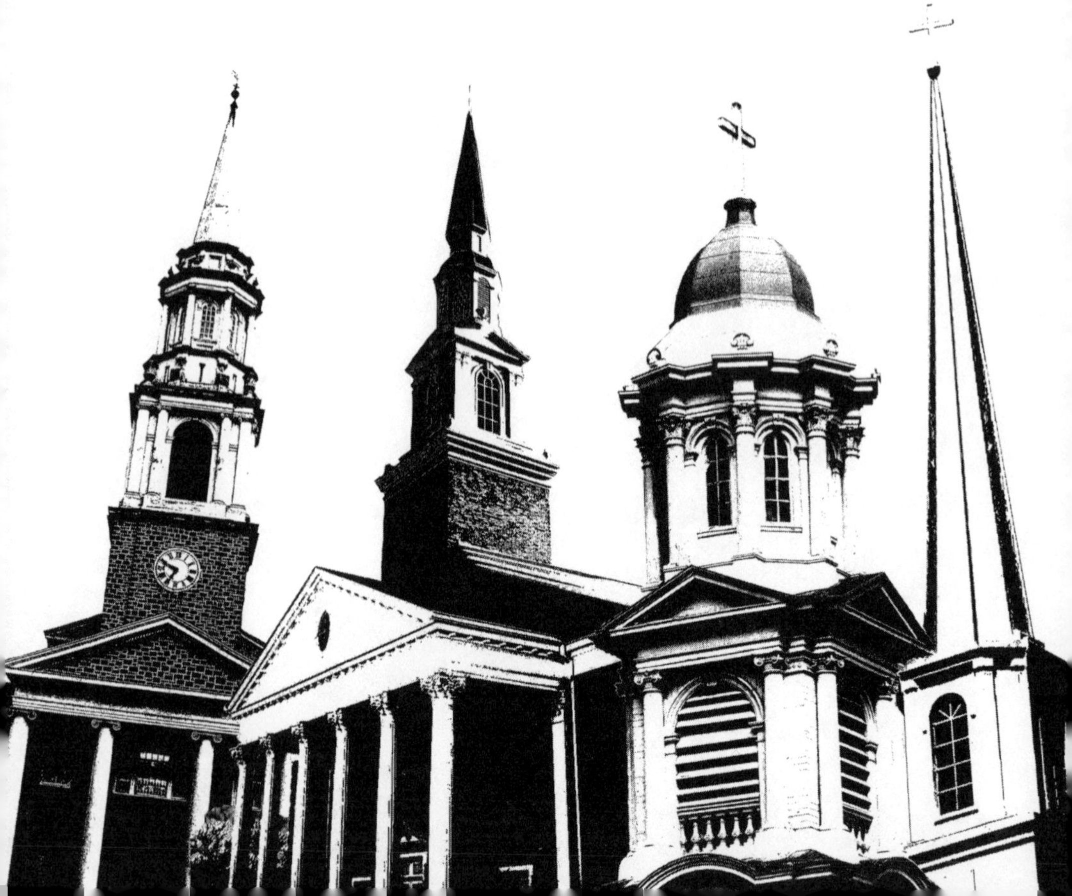

LEARNING beyond MY church TOGETHER

As we daily follow Jesus and grow to think and live beyond MY church, there will be much need of "detox" from the "MY church" addiction. To join the ongoing learning conversation as we sharpen one another to think and live "beyond MY church," visit:

www.beyondMYchurch.com

There will also be many stories to share. Stories of learning and living the ways of Jesus where you are and where you go, resulting in "on earth as it is in heaven." Send the stories happening among the local church expression of which you are a part, the stories happening in the unified church of the city where you live, and the stories happening among those who now believe in and know the One who was sent as a result of the unity of HIS church there at:

invitingconversation@gmail.com

Thanks!

1

And if you ever have a second, check out the following:

www.theChurchofWestOrange.com
www.ReproducingChurches.com
www.JasonCDukes.com
www.LiveSent.com
www.theworldwouldnotice.com
www.WestpointChurch.org
www.WorldCrafts.org
www.CMAresources.org
www.theforgottenways.org
www.ApostleFarm.com

And these are thrown in just for fun:
www.JellyTelly.com
http://www.youtube.com/watch?v=kjLygOK7V3I—the 10 Commandment Rap (my son is in it in the striped shirt!)

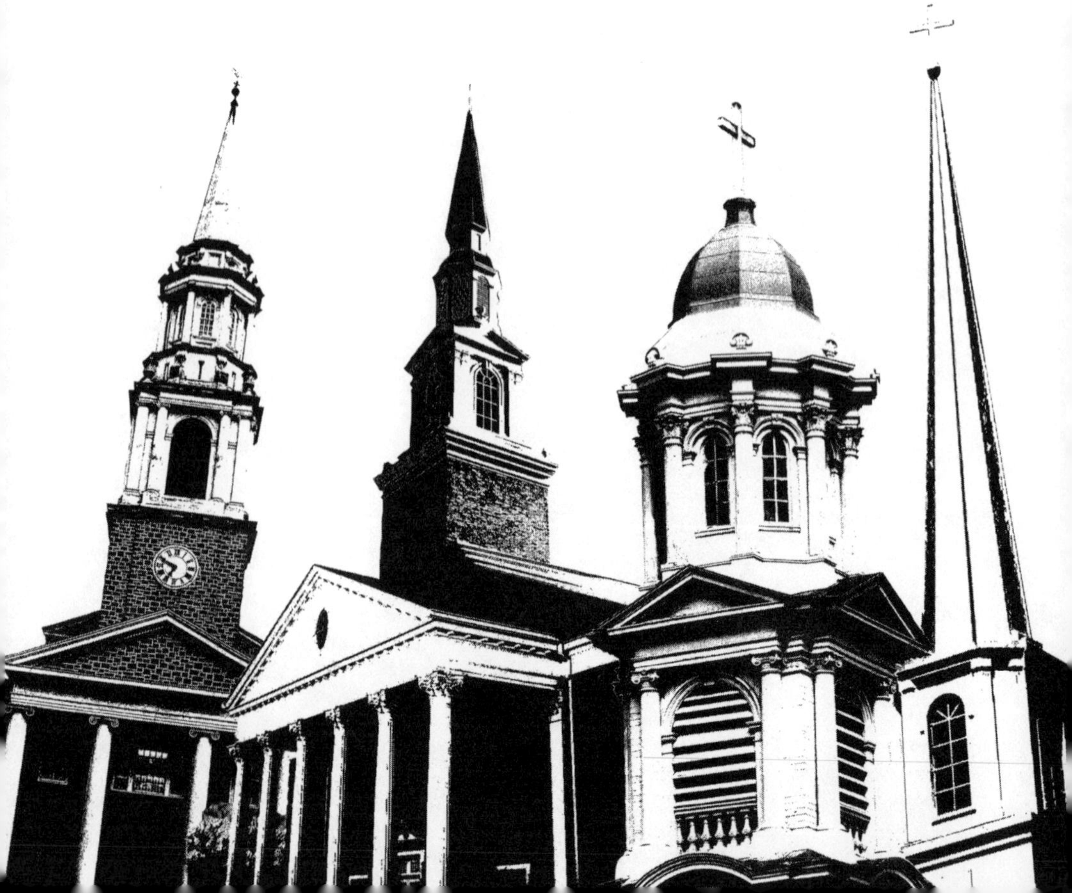

WE ARE UNITED

Register at www.beyondMYchurch.com, and we will send you a code for a free download of the song and video "We Are United." It is an original song and video from Jake Smith (www.JakeSmithMusic.com), Travis Manint, and my friends with Vintage Church NOLA (New Orleans, LA).

They are thinking and living "beyond MY church" and wanted to make this awesome song and video available to you. Enjoy.

CONTACT JASON:

_ invitingconversation@gmail.com
_ Twitter.com/jasoncdukes
_ Facebook.com/jasoncdukes
_ carrier pigeon to the west side of Orlando, Florida

Notes

Notes

Other resources for missional living by New Hope Publishers

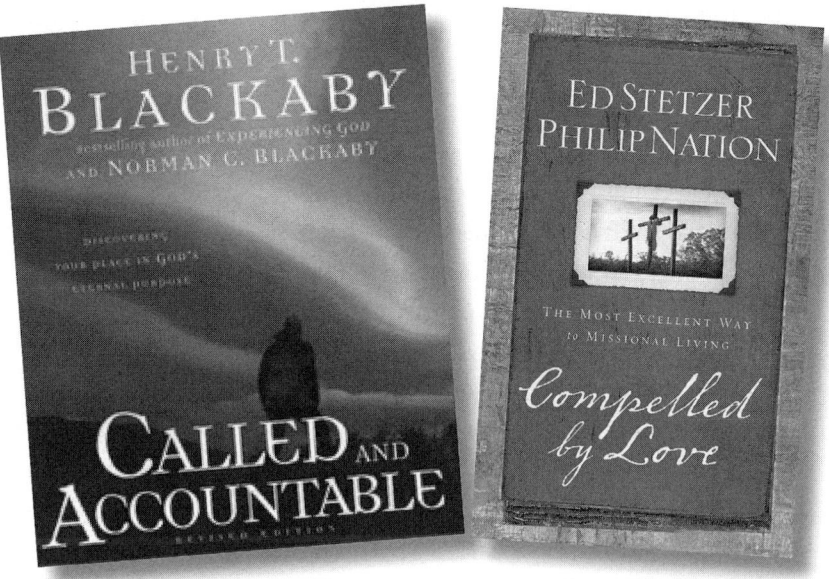

Called and Accountable
Discovering Your Place in God's Eternal Purpose
Henry T. Blackaby and
Norman C. Blackaby
ISBN-10: 1-59669-047-X
ISBN-13: 978-1-59669-047-9

Compelled by Love
The Most Excellent Way to Missional Living
Ed Stetzer and Philip Nation
ISBN-10: 1-59669-227-8
ISBN-13: 978-1-59669-227-5

Beyond Me
*Living a You-First Life
in a Me-First World*
Kathi Macias
ISBN-10: 1-59669-220-0
ISBN-13: 978-1-59669-220-6

NEW HOPE PUBLISHERS

Available in bookstores everywhere.

For information on these books or any New Hope product,
visit www.newhopedigital.com

New Hope® Digital is a division of WMU®, an international organization that challenges Christian believers to understand and be radically involved in God's mission.
For more information about WMU, go to www.wmu.com.
More information about New Hope books may be found at www.newhopedigital.com.
New Hope books may be purchased at your local bookstore.

Use the QR reader on your smartphone to visit us online at
www.newhopedigital.com

If you've been blessed by this book, we would like to hear your story. The publisher and author welcome your comments and suggestions at: newhopereader@wmu.org.